ROME'S ANATHEMAS:

INSIGHTS INTO THE PAPAL PANTHEON

Selwyn R. Stevens, Ph.D.

Published by:

© Selwyn R. Stevens, 2016

This book is copyright, apart from any fair dealing for the purpose of private study, research, criticism or review as permitted under the Copyright Act. Any part of this book which is reproduced by any means without the written permission of the Publisher would breach Biblical ethics and the law.

Additional copies of this book are available from many bookstores or from:

Jubilee Resources International Inc.

PO Box 3, Feilding 4740 New Zealand

or our secure Webshop at

www.jubileeresources.org

ISBN 978-1-87746389-1

All Scripture quotations in this book are from the

New King James - New Authorised Version, unless otherwise noted.

The author uses American English spelling, not the Queen's English.

Parts of this document were first published in "How to Minister to Change Lives and Communities," by Dr. Selwyn Stevens, published by Jubilee Resources International Inc., New Zealand. © 2006)

Special thanks to Dr. Robert Heidler (pages 23-29) & Vinnie Grace Holman (pages 71-75) for their excellent research inculded here, used by permission.

Contents

Truth: It's the New Hate Speech	4
Introduction	5
Mary's Command to Catholics	9
What are Curses?	19
The Emperor's New Church	23
The Church Gained a New Set of Holidays	27
The Cult of Isis	29
Who is "The Rock?"	33
What about the Fish?	37
Comparison Beliefs - Roman Catholic & The Bible	39
Evolution of Deception - Time-line of Roman Catholicism	47
Further Pagan Adoptions	51
Choices Must Be Made	59
Examples of False Teaching affecting Christians today	65
Pope John Paul says...	69
Another Example of False Teaching affecting Christians today	71
What about Infant Baptism?	77
What about the Sabbath?	79
Saints & Dead People	81
So, Who is Cursed?	85
Prayer of Release for Ex-Roman Catholics & their Descendents	87
About this author	96
Resources available by the same author	99

Truth - It's the new hate speech

"During times of universal deceit, telling the truth becomes a revolutionary act," so wrote George Orwell, author of "Animal Farm" & "1984."

Before we start, please pray through this prayer, for your own benefit.

Spiritual "Bolt-Cutter" Prayer

Dear Heavenly Father: I come to You in the name of the Lord Jesus Christ. And I renounce and turn from all lies, all preconceptions, deceptions, and self-deceptions, and all unteachableness that I or my ancestors have believed or entertained.

I confess them as my sins and I ask to be cleansed from them by the Blood of the Lord Jesus Christ. I renounce all vows of secrecy and silence about all ungodly activities.

I command every lying spirit, and every spirit of deception, self-deception, and unteachableness, and any other spirits associated with these sins to leave me now, harmlessly on my natural breathing, and not to return to me or to anyone whom I love, in the Name of the Lord Jesus Christ.

In the name of the Lord Jesus Christ, I come out of agreement with and renounce all shame, blame and guilt, all fear, all fear of failure, all fear of rejection, all fear of men, all fear of offending and ridicule, and all fear of not hearing God.

Lord Jesus, you are the Truth, and I surrender all these areas to Your Holy Spirit, Who is the Spirit of Truth, and whom You promised would lead me into all truth. In Jesus' Name. Amen.

Introduction

Some spiritual topics, regardless of how vexing they may become, must still be investigated and a Biblical understanding reached. There are many in the Protestant community who boldly claim that the Roman Catholic Church is every bit a cult, just like the Mormons and the Watchtower. On the other hand, the Church of Rome also has its defenders who have valid points to make. For one thing, I respect the official position the Roman Catholic Church has held to oppose abortion because they value life. They are also consistent in rejecting the concept of homosexual "marriage." Unfortunately, they have covered up too many pedophile priests who have abused children. So, it's not just about morality.

Our goal must be to become a part of the Kingdom of God, not part of a church regardless of its size or age. We can know that we are saved. We can be sure that when we die we will go directly to be with the Lord. If you don't know whether you are saved or not, you probably aren't. **"Examine yourselves as to whether you are in the faith. Test yourselves. Do you not know yourselves, that Jesus Christ is in you? - unless indeed you are disqualified,"** (2 Corinthians 13:5). "Jesus answered and said to him, **"Most assuredly, I say to you, unless one is born again, he cannot see the kingdom of God,"** (John 3:3) **"These things I have written to you who believe in the name of the Son of God, that you may know that you have eternal life, and that you may continue to believe in the name of the Son of God,"** (1 John 5:13).

To receive salvation, we must be born again and receive new life from God. If we have not been born again, we have not received salvation. If we truly have been born again we will be different than before. **"Therefore, if anyone is in Christ, he is a new creation; old things have passed away; behold, all things have become new,"** (2 Corinthians 5:17)

Please understand this crucial point: The Gospel is an ultimatum, not a message of diplomacy - you MUST be born again! That is God's requirement for entry into His heaven. Membership of a church does NOT guarantee this, regardless of which church.

Some years ago, I was asked by a pastor if and when I would address the issues of the curses from the Roman Catholic Church. I had previously studied and released teaching about other curses such as those from Masonic rituals, as well as some cult beliefs and practices. As I began to research this matter, I was increasingly concerned at what I was discovering. This is probably the least enjoyable topic I have ever had to research. I studied the issues over the Council of Trent held in the mid-1500's. Most non-Catholics have heard of Martin Luther, but know little of the Roman Catholic response to him and his revelation about grace and faith instead of religion. What also disturbed me was that this important topic isn't usually covered anymore in most Bible college or seminary training, so the level of ignorance is significant in pulpits, to say nothing of the pews.

It seemed necessary to locate and understand the origins of so many of the false teachings the Roman Catholic Church had adopted that were contrary to the Bible. My friend, Dr. Robert Heidler from Texas, had written a fascinating book entitled *"The Messianic Church Arising,"* so I asked him to come to New Zealand and teach this at our annual summer conferences. Part of Robert's teaching explained how Constantine shifted the church of that time towards Mithraism and anti-Semitism, and away from a Biblical faith.

About a decade ago I had written a paper on the Anathemas or curses from the Council of Trent. That paper was translated into Spanish by some keen former Roman Catholics from Latin America. At this time of writing, that paper has been translated into fifteen languages, so there is a clear hunger for more detailed material on this topic. This book is a consequence of that demand.

I remember being offered a large sum of money if I would continue my Unmasking series with "Unmasking Roman Catholicism." I declined (despite needing the money) because I am called to a positive ministry of Apologetics - including comparisons between religious/doctrinal beliefs and to explain the consequences of those choices. After all, when fully informed, every individual is answerable primarily to God - and not to some human authority. Had I accepted that generous offer, I would - to be consistent - have also had to "Unmask" the Anglicans/Episcopalians, Presbyterians, Lutherans, Methodists and many other denominations that have compromised with Freemasonry, New Age quasi-Christianity and some whose increasingly liberal views including their acceptance of "gay" ordination in total apostasy to the Bible? Where might one stop throwing bricks at other people? I personally don't find that approach helpful for the Kingdom of God, and the fruit is division where there needs to be sound Bible teaching to bring correction.

In my best-selling book, ***"Unmasking Freemasonry: Removing the Hoodwink,"*** I asked the question *"Can a Christian be a Freemason?"* Many Lodge members claim, *"Yes, they can."* I believe this is the wrong question. The most relevant question is, *"Should a Christian be a Freemason?"* After much research I have to state the answer is an emphatic *"No!"* I then presented compelling evidence as to why true Freemasonry and true Christianity are mutually exclusive. In my own country, some 85% of Freemasons have seen the real light and resigned from their lodge. In my city, five of their six lodge buildings have been closed to date.

The reason I mention this is because we should ask the same question of Roman Catholics. Can a Christian be a Roman Catholic? Yes, I know several who are born again, filled with the Holy Spirit, etc. Again, this is the wrong question. It should be *"Should a Christian be a Roman Catholic when so much official Catholic teaching is so contrary to the Bible?"* I trust this work will help answer that question for many people.

The true story is told of a young mother with an infant who boarded a train travelling across the vast plains of Canada one winter. The woman and baby were to get off in a remote station very late at night where some of her family would meet her and take them safely to their family home. As a blizzard was predicted during the journey, the supervisor on the train assured the woman he would ensure she got off at the correct stop.

Also on the train was an older woman who was very certain of what she knew, and who took a keen interest in the young woman and her infant. The older woman spoke of her knowledge of the trip and where all the stations were, although she hadn't made that journey for some years.

As the hours passed the younger woman and her infant slept. Very late at night, the older woman woke the sleeping younger woman, telling her that her stop was next and to prepare to get off with her baby. Shortly after, the train pulled into a remote station and the younger woman got off with her baby. There was no family there to collect her, but the older woman said they might be held up by the blizzard and to be patient and wait for their arrival. The train moved on.

About an hour later, the train supervisor came through the carriage to alert the younger woman that her stop was coming up in about 15 minutes. The older woman stated that the younger woman and child had gotten off at the previous stop because that was the right place. The supervisor knew better, and immediately called the engine driver to back the train up to rescue the young woman and her child. When they finally got to the station, the blizzard was blowing strongly, with snow drifts. They found the young mother and her baby frozen to death. It was the wrong stop. There was no help or family for her there.

The older woman was sincere, but she was sincerely wrong. It cost the lives of two innocent people.

God isn't interested in our sincerity, if it is sincerely wrong. What we need is truth. That's why we need God's Word, the Scriptures, to measure what we believe and do. That's also why Jesus is called "The Word," in the first chapter of John. That's why we need a reliable measure to help us avoid sincerely-held erroneous beliefs.

The Bible has historically been referred to as "the Canon," meaning it was the standard by which all Christian teaching and doctrine was to be measured against. After all, the Bible isn't a cafeteria where you can pick and choose what you want to believe.

Mary's Command to Catholics

By now, some Roman Catholics may be wondering if this is a "snow job" to discredit their church. No it's not. My purpose is to discover truth and separate it from error, using the Bible as the standard.

In the Gospel of St. John, we read of the marriage feast at Cana. Here Mary emphasizes the importance of Jesus and the words that He says. Realizing that the wine was gone and that she herself could not do anything, Mary tells Jesus, because He is the only One who could do something. Mary then gives the stewards a command, one that we must consider for us to be saved. Mary said, **"Whatever He say to you, do it!"**

These are the last recorded words of Mary, and the only passage in the Bible where Mary gives a command. It is therefore important for everyone, including for all Roman Catholics, to take heed to the words, **"Whatever He says to you, do it!"** Since the goal of all good Catholics is to get to heaven, let us look in the Bible and do what Mary said to do – read what Jesus says and do it.

Jesus says He is the only one that can save and be our saviour. **"I am the way, the truth and the life. No one comes to the Father except through Me,"(John 14:6).**

The Bible also says that Jesus is the only Mediator between God and man (1 Timothy 2:5), and it is only through Him that we have access to God the Father, (Ephesians 2:18).

Jesus never said to trust in saints, the sacraments, the Pope or Mary to save us. The Bible says **"Salvation is found in no one else, for there is no other name under heaven given to men (than Jesus) by which we must be saved," (Acts 4:12).**

Only Jesus can save us! Jesus never said for us to make special sacrifices or do good works in order to be saved. He did say **"But to him who does not work but believes on Him who justifies the ungodly,**

Mary painted as a deity - the Queen of Heaven - see Jeremiah 7:17-19

his faith is accounted as righteousness," (Romans 4:5).

"For it is by grace you have been saved, through faith – and this not from ourselves, it is the gift of God – not by works, lest anyone should boast," (Ephesians 2:8-9).

And: "That if you confess with your mouth, "Jesus is Lord," and believe in your heart that God raised Him from the dead, you will be saved. For it is with your heart that you believe and are justified, and it is with your mouth that you confess and are saved," (Romans 10:9-10).

Jesus says that God's words are the only authority to follow: **"He that rejects me, and receives not my words, has one that judges him: the word that I have spoken, the same shall judge him in the last day." (John 12:48).**

Jesus did not say that traditions or the rules of men could be added to His words. Instead He said, **"They worship Me in vain; their teachings are but rules taught by men. You have let go of the commands of God and are holding on to the traditions of men... You have a fine way of setting aside the commands of God in order to observe your own traditions! ...Thus you nullify the word of God by your tradition that you have handed down. And you do many things like that," (Mark 7:7-9, 13).**

It must be pointed out that the Bible, God's Word, clearly curses anyone who adds to or takes away from the Word of God - the Holy Bible, (See Revelation 22:18; John 10:35; Deuteronomy 4:2 & 12:32; & Proverbs 30:5-6). This means that God has cursed the

Roman Catholic Church because they have adopted doctrine and practise that He opposes. This includes the idolization of Mary, instead of simply obeying this one command she made in real life!

You can know that you are saved and have eternal life if you put your complete faith in Jesus Christ, and stop relying on yourself, the church, the sacraments or any other works. Jesus is the only way to heaven. Jesus said, **"I write these things to you who believe in the name of the Son of God so that you may know that you have eternal life,"** (1 John 5:13). Did you read that carefully? You can KNOW that you have eternal life, but only through your acceptance of Jesus, based on His terms. This has nothing to do with Mary.

I believe it may be helpful to check out the following chart, used by permission of the publishers of the *Christian Research Journal*. This was published along with a series of five articles on the Church of Rome, under the series title, *"What Think Ye of Rome?"*

This picture is the Mystical Catholic Heaven by a Catholic artist. The 2nd Vatican Council stated, *"We believe the multitude of those souls gathered around Jesus and Mary in Paradise forms the Heavenly Church."* But the Heavenly Father is not on the throne, and Jesus is supported by Mary, the only adult on the throne! This is a picture based on false teaching.

The standard by which others were measured was the Evangelical Bible perspective, and the Roman Catholic Church, the Jehovah's

Witnesses, Latter-Day Saints (Mormons) and the United Pentecostal Church were compared with that standard. A word about definitions: Affirm means "Declare to be True"; Deny means "Declare untrue"; Distort means "Negative Alteration"; & Compromise means "Unacceptable Concession."

Doctrine	RC	JW	LDS	UPC
All theistic attributes of God	Affirm	Deny	Deny	Distort
Triune Nature of God	Affirm	Deny	Deny	Deny
Personality of the Holy Spirit	Affirm	Deny	Distort	Distort
Two natures of Christ	Affirm	Deny	Distort	Distort
Virgin Birth	Affirm	Affirm	Distort	Affirm
Justified by Faith	Comp.	Deny	Deny	Comp.
Christ's Atonement Sufficient	Comp.	Deny	Deny	Distort
Christ's Bodily Resurrection	Affirm	Deny	Affirm	Affirm
Eternal Conscious punishment	Affirm	Deny	Distort	Affirm
Literal Return of Christ	Affirm	Distort	Distort	Affirm
Immortal Soul	Affirm	Deny	Distort	Affirm
Inerrant Bible	Affirm	Distort	Deny	Distort
Authority of Bible	Comp.	Comp.	Comp.	Comp.
Continuity of the Church	Affirm	Deny	Deny	Deny
Predestination	Affirm	Deny	Deny	Deny
Salvation Outside their church	Comp.	Deny	Comp.	Comp.
Eternal Life in Heaven	Affirm	Distort	Distort	Affirm
Final Judgement	Affirm	Distort	Distort	Affirm

(Source: Christian Research Journal, Spring 1993)

It needs to be stated very clearly that we personally know many Roman Catholics who are born-again and spirit-filled, and these people hold doctrinal views largely indistinguishable from the Scriptures and we must regard them as brothers and sisters in Christ. The fruit of the Holy Spirit is evident, including their life-style choices. Many of these brethren have been told by God to stay in their church and share the truth of the Gospel of Jesus Christ with those around them. God is sovereign, and if He wishes to call and commission some people to do this for Him, who are we to deny God's call?

Those who have either left the Roman Catholic Church or who

were never part of it need to be careful they don't fall into self-righteousness when criticizing Born-again Catholic Christians. All Roman Catholics have a right to hear the Gospel, as have all Mormons, Jehovah's Witnesses, Atheists and Freemasons!

The article mentioned above by the CRI Journal asked the provocative question, *"Is the Church of Rome a Cult?"* The considered answer is both revealing, and we believe, correct: *"We don't believe the Church of Rome is a cult (using the usual definitions): we do believe it is an historic Christian denomination in desperate need of Biblical Correction."*

It would be helpful to understand something of the make-up of the Roman Catholic Church, as it is not one stream, but many flowing together, as shown below. In their book, *"Protestants and Catholics - Do they now agree?"* Dr. John Ankerberg and Dr. John Weldon (Harvest House Publishing) provide one of the better explanations of the different streams within the Roman Catholic Church. I have summarized these so you can see understand this. Not all Roman Catholics would agree with these labels, but they are appropriate, fair and reasonable.

1. Nominal or social Catholic - those who are largely uncommitted, probably born into or married into the Roman Catholic Church, but with little understanding of the theology of the Church. In practice they are Catholics in name only. The Church regards them as members because of their "baptism."

2. Syncretistic or eclectic Catholics - those parts of the church which have combined or absorbed elements of pagan religions to varying degrees, especially in South America and Africa.

3. Traditional or Orthodox Catholics - the powerful conservative stream within the church which holds to papal authority, historic church doctrines such as those enacted at the Council of Trent. It can also include those who reject the abandonment of the Latin Mass, etc. and all other liberalism.

4. Moderate Catholics - those primarily post-Second Vatican Council, neither totally traditional nor entirely liberal.

5. Modernist liberal Catholics - the post-Second Vatican Council "progressives that reject traditional doctrine to varying degrees.

6. Ethnic or cultural Catholics - often migrants to countries such as America, Australia, etc., who feel that not to be a Catholic is not to belong, hence to lose their nationality and cultural roots.

7. Lapsed or apostate Catholics - those backslidden, indifferent or alienated from the Church.

8. Charismatic Catholics - primarily those who seek the Baptism of the Holy Spirit, along with speaking in tongues, healing, prophetic utterance and other spiritual gifts. This group has a much greater emphasis on Scripture than Church tradition.

9. Mystical Catholics - (some wrongly link this group with 8 above) those who are drawn to the mystical and not infrequently the occult writings and experiences of Catholic mystics in the past.

10. "Evangelical" Catholics - usually former Protestant Evangelicals who often retain many of their former beliefs but who now accept the Church of Rome as the 'One True Church,' and its doctrines authoritative.

11. Evangelical "Catholics" - those Roman Catholics who have rejected all unbiblical teachings from Rome, but remaining within the Church to evangelize other Roman Catholics and to help bring reform to their Church.

With this in mind there are several issues that affect many present and former Roman Catholics, and we would be failing in love and duty if we neglected to spell these out for the stated purpose of the spiritual and emotional freedom of all concerned.

It is recognized there are many in the Roman Catholic Church who hold views or have different practices from those promulgated by their Church authorities. One of the primary sources of difficulty are the Anathemas of the Council of Trent. Briefly the Council of Trent was an ecumenical council of the Church of Rome, held in the city of Trent in northern Italy between 1545 and 1563. It was the official Roman Catholic Church response to the challenge of the Protestant Reformation started by Martin Luther, a Catholic priest who discovered how far the church had wandered from the Bible. Pope Pius 4th formally confirmed all the decrees of this council in 1564.

The Council of Trent

The Greek word **"Anathema"** means a curse - the disfavor or judgement of God. A Scriptural example would be Galatians 1:8-9, where *"The Apostle (Paul) declares in the strongest manner that the Gospel he preached was the one and only way of salvation and that to preach another was to nullify the death of Christ."* (Vines p. 262.) Twice Paul proclaims that if anyone, whether angel or man, brings any other competing message of salvation, let him be "anathema" - accursed!

Let us apply this to today. The Mormons teach that to be "Born Again" is to be baptized into their church (as opposed to the Kingdom of God). On the other hand the Jehovah's Witnesses teach that by good works and becoming a Jehovah's Witness one may achieve some form of salvation that cannot be guaranteed. Both these examples fall under the Anathema of the Apostle Paul.

A small number of the Canons or statements of the Council of Trent would be agreed with by Christians. One example is Canon 1 recorded in Chapter 16 on Justification, and approved on 13 January 1547 during the sixth session. This canon states *"If anyone says that man can be justified before God by his own works, whether done by his own natural powers or through the teaching of the law, without divine grace through Jesus Christ, let him be anathema."*

Unfortunately many of the remaining 17 canons in that chapter compromise the issue of Justification by grace through faith in Jesus Christ. It was that very verse which was Martin Luther's first major revelation, and which caused him to reject indulgences and the many other corrupt practices that he had been involved in as a priest in the church of that time.

Under the Canons on Sacraments (17th Session, 3 March 1547) Canon 10 states, *"If anyone says that all Christians have the power to administer the word and all the sacraments, let him be anathema."* In effect this prohibits all but ordained Roman Catholic priests from preaching the word and leading the Lord's Supper/Communion/Eucharist and baptism, etc. (These last two being the only sacraments instituted by Jesus). This is clearly not acceptable to Bible-believing Christians. Despite the infrequency of teaching on it, there is the well-established doctrine of the Priesthood of All Believers. This is covered below: in 1 Peter 2, and Revelation 1. God Himself states that no church authority has the right to over-rule the Scriptures.

"But you are a chosen race, a royal priesthood, a holy nation, a people for his own possession, that you may proclaim the excellencies of him who called you out of darkness into his marvellous light. Once you were not a people, but now you are God's people; once you had not received mercy, but now you have received mercy," (1 Peter 2:9-10).

"...and made us a kingdom, priests to his God and Father, to him be glory and dominion forever and ever. Amen," (Revelation 1:6).

Canon 4 states that anyone who denies baptism of a newly born infant is *"baptized for the remission of sin"* invokes an anathema.

Canon 5 states, *"Baptism is necessary for Salvation."* We have criticized cults for similar false statements. Baptism in the New Testament is a command of the Lord Jesus, and its purpose is obedience leading to sanctification. Nowhere is it taught as a Salvation issue. To be baptized, there are two requirements in Scripture - the person must be old enough to confess their total faith and trust in Jesus Christ, and it must be accompanied with genuine repentance for all sin and acceptance of the sacrifice of Jesus on Calvary's cross.

There are people who have died following conversion but prior to baptism. Does God's grace not cover this? Even the thief on the cross was offered Paradise that day - and there is no record he was baptized while he was nailed to a cross along-side that of Jesus. Bible-believing Christians also reject infant baptism because an infant or small child is too young to recognise their spiritual condition before God. New Testament baptism requires repentance to be meaningful. An infant may be dedicated to God with water (either sprinkling or plunging) but that doesn't constitute baptism. Children are sanctified by their parent's spiritual state until they reach an age of knowledge and awareness (somewhere between 8 and 14 years of age).

For the sake of space here, I will mention only two other Anathemas. During the 4th Session affirmed on 8th April, 1546, it is declared anathema to all who reject the Apocryphal books. Since these were never quoted by Jesus Christ (whereas virtually all Old Testament books were) and since the Apocryphal books have notable errors of fact, they have always been rejected by the Councils of the early church whose task it was to discern true Scripture from sub-standard or false, when compiling the 66 books of the Bible. The Apocryphal books failed the many tests to qualify as Scriptural canon.

Later in the same session, it was announced that only the Church of Rome could interpret Holy Scripture; and further that the printing of any book on *"sacred doctrinal matters"* *"without permission from ecclesiastical superiors"* also invoked anathema. With the exception of the Vulgate version, all Bible translations and commentaries etc. invoke this anathema/curse. This view is highly objectionable to all Christians.

Much has happened since the 1540's. Did the Second Vatican Council during the 1960's deal with these contentious issues? According to "Vatican Council 2" (printed by Costello Publishing Co, Northport New York, General Editor Austin Flannery O.P., with Nihil Obstat and Imprimatur included, vol. 1 1984, & vol. 2 1982.) Yes it did. # 46 states "This Sacred Council ... proposes **again** the decrees of the Second Council of Nicea, of the Council of Florence, **and of the Council of Trent.**" (Vol. 1, p. 412).

These are just a few of many statements that the Roman Catholic Church authorities deem unchangeable. If such teaching or practise is contrary to Scripture, is it possible these invoke God's Anathema? I believe so on the basis of objective Biblical truth. What is required is for Roman Catholic Christians to write to their leaders and promote Bible doctrines and request removal of all anti-Bible doctrines of their church.

This picture is a false representation of Mary by a Catholic artist. She never had rosary beads - they are a Hindu invention, also later adopted by Buddhism, Islam, & later by Catholics.

What are Curses?

Let's check this term *"Anathema"* - its etymology is late Latin anathemat-, anathema, from Greek, a thing devoted to evil, curse, from anatithenai to set up, dedicate, from ana- + tithenai to place, set:

1 a: One that is cursed by ecclesiastical authority;

b: Someone or something intensely disliked or loathed;

2 a: A ban or curse solemnly pronounced by ecclesiastical authority and accompanied by excommunication;
b: The denunciation of something as accursed
c: a vigorous denunciation;

3: A person or thing accursed or consigned to damnation or destruction.

Based on Scripture and personal experience, a curse is being empowered to fail, while a blessing is being empowered to succeed! Curses are words empowered by an evil spirit, unless the curse is spoken by God Himself. In that case, God dispatches angels to do His bidding. According to 2 Chronicles 18, God also uses demons to the same end.

Here is a sample: *"Pius, bishop, servant of the servants of God, for the perpetual memory hereof... I recognize the Holy Catholic and Apostolic Roman Church as the mother and mistress of all churches; and I promise and swear true obedience to the Roman pontiff,* **successor of St. Peter, prince of the apostles, and vicar of Jesus Christ**. *All other things also delivered, defined, and declared by the sacred canons and ecumenical councils, and particularly by the holy Synod of Trent, I undoubtingly receive and profess, and at the same time all things contrary, and any heresies soever condemned by the Church, and rejected and* **anathematized**, *I, in like manner, condemn, reject, and anathematize.*

*This true Catholic faith, **outside of which no one can be saved,** which at present I readily profess and truly hold, I, (Name) promise, vow, and swear, that I will most steadfastly retain and confess the same entire and undefiled to the last breath of life (with God's help), and that I will take care, as far as shall be in my power, that it be held, taught, and preached by my subjects, or those whose charge shall devolve on me in virtue of my office. So help me God, and these holy gospels of God." (emphasis added)*

Let's understand another term: **Sorcery** is defined by Webster's Dictionary as, *"1. The use of power gained from the assistance or control of evil spirits, especially for divining; necromancy, & 2. Magic."*

Tyndale's Bible Dictionary defines magic as the *"attempt to influence or control people or events through supernatural forces. These forces are called upon by means of ceremonies, the recitation of spells, charms, incantations, and other forms of ritual."*

Roman Catholics are told they must believe some things under coercion. When Rome dogmatizes a doctrine it becomes a demand under threat of being anathematized or cursed. An example will show this. At the Council of Trent (reaffirmed at the Second Vatican Council in 1967) Session 8 number 844 states:

*"If anyone shall say that the sacraments of the New Law were not all instituted by Jesus Christ our Lord, or that there are more or less than seven, namely baptism, confirmation, Eucharist, penance, extreme unction, order and matrimony, or even that anyone of these seven is not truly and strictly speaking a sacrament: let him be **anathema**."*

"This is a curse meant to damn one to hell. The (Bible)... uses the final phrase literally once, **"If any man love not the Lord Jesus Christ, let him be anathema, Maranatha,"** *(1 Corinthians 16:22). The last two terms are transliterated Greek meaning "accursed" and "Our Lord Come!" The way "accursed" is used in Scripture means to be delivered up to the judicial wrath of God. Paul used*

the term five times. Two of them refer to Jesus (Galatians 3:13; 1 Corinthians 12:3). One is in reference to himself on behalf of Israel (Romans 9:23). One is used for a person with no love for God (1 Corinthians 16:22), and one in reference to someone who preaches a false Gospel, (Galatians 1:8-9)... The Apostle Paul had this authority but when one typically thinks of a person who frequently practices pronouncing curses on another human being, witchcraft and sorcery come to mind. The Romanists (The Roman Catholic Church) have pronounced more curses on people who disagree with them than any institution on the face of the earth. We firmly believe that Rome's traditions and rituals are sorcerous."
("Petrus Romanus" by Thomas Horn & Chris Putnam, p 295)

Following official Roman Catholic doctrine, Catholic artists portray Jesus as still in the Cross while the good news is that He has risen!

The Emperor's New Church: Where did it all begin to go wrong?

Constantine came to the Roman throne with the announcement that he was now a follower of Christ. When Constantine saw his vision of the cross in the sky next to the sun, he evidently assumed Jesus was manifestation of Mithras. The Christians could hardly believe it. The ecclesia had been through three centuries of persecution. The reign of the Emperor Diocletian (287-305) had been called the "Age of Martyrs."

Now a new Emperor claimed to be a follower of Jesus. This seemed an answer to prayer. The persecution ended. Christianity changed from illegal to a favored religion. It became socially acceptable and even popular, to be a Christian. The emperor gave extravagant gifts to prominent citizens who converted. Sunday was made an official Roman holiday. Constantine built magnificent church buildings. Many Christian leaders hailed Constantine as a New Apostle. There was a major problem: Constantine not only legalized Christianity, he tried to improve it.

In return for his favor, Constantine demanded control. He claimed the title **"Pontifex Maximus"** – interestingly the title of the High Priest of Mithras. Other pagan additions were adopted, including Dagon's mitre.

In the year AD 325 Constantine called, and presided over, the first general council of the church, the Council of Nicea. His purpose was to reorganize the church and give it a new image.

Constantine literally reinvented Christianity. Christianity after Nicea was a different religion than Christianity before Nicea. Beginning with Constantine and through the dark ages, Christianity was cut off from it's Hebrew roots through persistent and brutal persecution by an anti-Semitic church leadership. The church today still suffers because of the things we have lost. One definite sign is the curse of division by denominations.

Let's look at some of the things that changed:

1. Death of House Ecclesia

St. John Lateran

Shortly after his "conversion" Constantine built the first "church" building in Rome, St. John Lateran, a Roman basilica. It was patterned after the imperial palace. To the Romans, the imperial throne room was the ultimate place of worship. Emperors were worshipped as gods. Constantine used this as the pattern for Christian worship. Basilica-type church buildings were built all over the empire.

Constantine then enacted a law that "houses of prayer" must be abolished, and forbidding Christians from holding Ecclesia in private homes, as was their custom. This was worded *"to strike terror into the minds of his subjects."*

2. A Change in Worship

Constantine decided to improve the way the Christians worshipped. Less than one year after his conversion: he stated *"I am going to make plain to them what kind of worship is to be offered to God... What higher duty have I as emperor than to cause all to offer God true religion and due worship."*

To Constantine's Roman/pagan mind, the highest expression of worship was found in the solemn rituals of the Roman Imperial court with solemn ceremonies with fixed written forms of worship and the burning of incense and the carrying of candles, and similar rituals.

3. Rejection of the Ecclesia's Hebrew Roots

Like many Romans, Constantine hated the Hebrews. He called them *"A conquered people, hostile to Rome."* Constantine decided to purge his new church of Hebrew elements. He commanded the church to avoid following customs of the Hebrews, such as outlawing the Biblical Feasts and Sabbaths.

His Decree at Nicea (325) *"Let us have nothing in common with the Jews, who are our adversaries... this irregularity [observing Passover] must be corrected."*

Eusebius added: *"It appeared an unworthy thing that we should follow practises of the Jews... Let us withdraw ourselves from all participation in their baseness.... All should unite in avoiding all participation in the conduct of the Jews."*

Bernard Lazare describes changes resulting from Nicea: *"[Before Nicea] Christians attended the synagogues, [and] celebrated the Jewish holidays... It required the action of the Nicaean Council to free Christianity of this last bond by which it had still been tied to its cradle."*

Those who observed Biblical feasts were marked "anathema" (cut off or accursed). This eventually became a crime against the state, punishable by death.

Church Attempts to Enforce Nicea's Decree

The Council of Antioch (A.D. 345) – *"If any bishop, presbyter or deacon will dare, after this decree, to celebrate Passover with the Jews, the council judges them to be anathema from the church. This council not only deposes them from ministry, but also any others who dare to communicate with them."*

The Council of Laodicea (A.D. 365) - *"It is not permitted to receive festivals which are by Jews, nor to hold a festival together with them. (Canon 37) Christians must not Judaize by resting on the Sabbath, but must work on that day... but if any be found to be Judaizes let them be Anathema (cursed) from Christ."* (Apart from the obvious Anti-Semitism, this breaks the Fourth Commandment.)

The Council of Agde, France (506) – *"Clerics must not take part in Jewish festivals."*

The 2nd Council of Nicea (787) – *"[Those who] openly or secretly keep the Sabbath and follow other practices in the manner of the Jews are not to be received into communion, nor into prayer, nor into the church."*

The fact that so many pronouncements were made over hundreds of years against involvement in Sabbaths, the Feasts of the Lord, etc., indicates how deeply entrenched God's commands were amongst those who wanted to remain obedient to Him, despite such an desperate attempts to get rid of them.

Constantine divorced the church from its Hebrew Roots. But more than that: He married the church to Paganism!

Constantine put a picture of Mithras on his coins. These coins dated two years after his claimed conversion! On his triumphal arch, built to celebrate his victory over Maxentius, he put a picture of Mithras.

In AD 321, Constantine honoured his newfound faith by making Sunday a state holiday, but in his decree Constantine designated this new holiday: proclaiming it *"the Venerable Day of the Sun."* So when the claimed "Christian" emperor made the Christian day of worship a State holiday, he named it for the pagan sun god!

Constantine's confusion over the identity of Jesus seems to have infected many of the unconverted pagans now crowding into the church. In the fourth century, a Roman mosaic shows Jesus as the sun god driving a chariot across the sky.

By the fifth century, it became a common practise for worshippers to turn and bow down to the rising sun in the East before entering Saint Peter's basilica in Rome. This influx of pagan thinking affected the church in a number of ways.

The Church Gained a New Set of Holidays.

Before Constantine, the holidays of the Ecclesia were the Biblical Feasts. The Ecclesia never had a celebration for birth of Jesus – it wasn't important.

But the Romans celebrated the December 25th as the birthday of Mithras. (In AD 274 the emperor Aurelian had made it a state holiday.)

The unconverted pagans rushing into the church didn't want to give up their holiday. They declared December 25th to be the birthday of Christ, and gave the church a new holiday called Christmas.

There was another new holiday: the Spring Fertility Festival!

Pagans held feast in spring to honor the goddess of fertility, whose symbol was an egg.

Canaanites: called her ASHERAH.
Persians: called her AESTARTE.
Babylonians: called her ISHTAR.
Britons: called her EASTRE

Constantine outlawed Passover, and ordered Christians to celebrate Christ's resurrection at the time of the spring fertility festival instead.

Christ's resurrection was taken out of its Biblical context and celebrated in the context of a pagan feast.

By the end of the fourth century, Pagan sacrifices were outlawed and pagan temples were turned into churches. Pagan shrines were changed into Christian shrines. Some pagan priests even became Christian priests. Pagans were told that they lived in a Christian empire and it was their responsibility to live as Christians.

The trouble is, they didn't know Jesus. They were still pagans. Their beliefs had not changed. They responded to the official decrees by giving "Christian" names to pagan gods and continuing to worship as they had before. Pagans didn't mind changing the names of their gods.

When the Greek religion came to Rome, the Greek gods were given Roman names!

ZEUS	became	JUPITER
HERA	=	JUNO
POSEIDON	=	NEPTUNE
ATHENA	=	MINERVA
APHRODITE	=	VENUS
ARES	=	MARS

When pagan worship was outlawed, pagans changed the names again!

The Cult of Isis

Isis was the Egyptian goddess, often called: "Great Virgin" and "Mother of God." It is usually seen holding the child Horus. Worshippers of Isis began calling Isis by the name "Mary." In this way they could continue to legally worship Isis.

Worshippers of other pagan gods used the names of Christian saints and martyrs. If you are a pagan farmer and told you can no longer go to your temple and pray to the god of Harvest, what would you do?

You go to the church building that used to be your temple and pray to the patron Saint of Harvest!

If you were a musician, you weren't allowed to pray to the goddess of music; you would pray to Saint Cecelia, the patron saint of music.

If you were a soldier, you could no longer pray to Mars, the god of war; now you would pray to Michael, patron saint of war.

And if you were a mother, you can't pray to Hera, protector of families; but instead you'd pray to Saint Anne, patron saint of families.

They still called it "The Church" but it was all just paganism. Your worship hasn't changed.

You are simply calling your gods by different names.

- By the year 600, paganism had inundated the church.

- Most of the church's leaders were unbelievers.

- Those resisting were persecuted as enemies of the empire.

- By the Middle Ages not only the common people, but even many kings and priests, were illiterate. Even those who could read were often denied access to the Bible. Bibles were written in a language people couldn't understand and chained to the pulpit where they couldn't be read.

- Superstition and idolatry were rampant.

- Salvation was by good works, pilgrimages, and financial contributions.

- The Church became a powerful and wealthy political organization.

"Things changed drastically with Constantine. He ordered the building of St. Peter's and St. Paul's basilicas, and he bequeathed the Lateran Palace to Pope Sylvester. In the West, the title "pope" was largely reserved to the city of Rome when Leo the Great (440-461) infamously assumed the historic pagan title of Pontifex Maximus favored by Emperor Constantine. In the eighth century, the papacy broke with the Eastern emperor and allied itself with a Western royal and claimed land in central Italy for political autonomy... Throughout the early Middle Ages (600-1050), the Eastern and Western Church honored the bishop of Rome as the "vicar of St. Peter," but the East ignored him for all intents and purposes and the Western Emperors only paid attention when it was expedient.

During the Middle Ages, the titles "Vicar of St. Peter," "Vicar of the Prince of the Apostles," and "Vicar of the Apostolic See" were all employed interchangeably. It was only in the eleventh century that Gregory 7th made "Pope" or "Pontiff" the official title. Accordingly, the term "papacy" originated in the later eleventh century to differentiate the Roman bishop from the bishops of all other diocese. During this time political manoeuvres allowed the Church to assert more and more worldly power. In the thirteenth century, largely due to Pope Innocent 3rd, the Pontifex Maximus asserted the priority of the spiritual over the material world and adopted the supercilious new title of "Vicar of Christ." This renders into English literally as "instead of Christ." Of course, to one with a coherent Biblical world-view, this seems **outrageously blasphemous.** *"* ("Petrus Romanus" by Thomas Horn & Chris Putnam, p 172).

The Vatican's Coat of Arms (shown) include the crossed keys they claim to represent Simon Peter. The keys are gold and silver to represent the power to loose and bind. Since there is no Biblical evidence Peter ever visited Rome, let alone started a church there, this is based on a fraud. The triple crown or tiara are said to symbolize the triple power of the Pope as "father of kings," "governor of the world" and "Vicar of Christ." Clearly, world domination is the goal.

Historically the Bishops of Rome claimed a position of power and prestige that has never been theirs. The Eternal City – the City of God - is not Rome, but Jerusalem. Rome is the "Eternal City" of Mithraism.

Even the name of this church is an oxymoron: 'Roman' means from Rome, the city; 'Catholic' means universal (because they adopted pagan influences from everywhere); and 'Church' is a circle for pagan ritual (with Masonic and other occult meanings, because of a mistranslation of 'Ecclesia' from Greek and 'Knesset' in Hebrew. The term Ecclesia should be translated "assembly" or "congregation." In other words, a gathering of people, not a building or geographical place. Space precludes further elaboration here).

The head of the universal Ecclesia is Jesus Christ alone. (His original Hebrew name and title are Yeshua Ben Yahweh.)

Who is the "Rock"?

"And I also say to you that you are Peter, and on this rock I will build My ecclesia, and the gates of Hades shall not prevail against it. 19 "And I will give you the keys of the kingdom of heaven, and whatever you bind on earth will be bound in heaven, and whatever you loose on earth will be loosed in heaven," (Matthew 16:18-19).

"For the sake of argument, even if we were to grant that Peter is the Rock in Matthew 16:18, it still would not make him a Pontifex Maximus. The same authority Jesus gave to Peter (Matthew 16:18) is also given to all the apostles, (Matthew 16:18). Paul also affirms the Church is, **"built upon the foundation of the apostles and prophets, Jesus Christ Himself being the chief cornerstone,"** *(Ephesians 2:20)... It is also telling that Catholic apologists seldom mention that only a few verses later Jesus rebukes Peter as Satan:* **"Get behind Me, Satan: you are an offence to Me: for you are not mindful of the things of God, but the things of men,"** *(Matthew 16:23). No one gives Peter superiority in apostasy because of this condemnation, thus it seems wise we not give him supremacy in the ecclesia for commendation."* ("Petrus Romanus" by Thomas Horn & Chris Putnam, p 175-6)

"While Peter was an important apostle, he was no more preeminent than Paul. Peter helped establish the church in Jerusalem, but it was James, the brother of Jesus who assumed the leadership of the Jerusalem church, (Acts 15). Paul was the apostle to the gentiles, (Acts 14; 16-28) while Peter became the apostle to the Jews, (see Galatians 2:7-8).

Regarding Peter, he had a wife living in Capernaum (Matthew 8:14), and there is no Biblical reference to him ever having traveled to Rome. The Book of Acts chronicles the Apostles activities, following the death of Jesus. Peter was preaching in Jerusalem as late as 45AD, (Acts 12) and was last recorded as being at the Council of Jerusalem about 48 or 49 AD. There is no record of Peter having been bishop of Rome when he was clearly recorded as remaining in Israel/Palestine (Palestine was the Roman name for the province the locals knew as Israel). The real question is whether we believe the Bible record or third century Catholic tradition?

"Peter did not found the Roman (Christian) community, and there is no good evidence that that community had a bishop – an 'overseer' - in the First century." (Thomas F.X. Noble, "Lecture One: What is Papal History & How did it begin?" notes for course Popes and the papacy: a History" The Teaching Company 2006, page 3)

The New Testament evidence simply doesn't support the official Catholic history.

When the Roman Empire crumbled, the Roman Church stepped in to fill the vacuum, becoming a great military power. I appreciate the true story of Francis of Assisi, who later in life was invited to the Vatican. The pope of the time gave Francis a guided tour of his palace and with a sweep of his hand proclaimed, "You can see, Francis, no longer can we say "silver and gold have I none." To which, Francis replied, "Yes your holiness, but we also can no longer say, "Arise and walk." The Christians in Constantine's church had lost the supernatural power of God it had once known, as shown in the Book of Acts.

"Traditionally Romanists base their case primarily on this passage, claiming that Peter is the "rock" upon which the Church is founded, thus giving his successors the full power of binding and loosing. There is certainly a word-play evident in the Greek. The name Peter is 'Petros' and rock is 'Petras.' Even so it is not clear in the original language that Christ was referring to Peter being the foundation of the Church when He spoke of "this rock." "Peter" is in the second person but "this rock" is in the third person. Furthermore, "Peter" is a masculine singular term, but "rock" is a feminine singular term. Thus, it seems unlikely that they have the same referent. Jesus could easily have said "and upon you the rock," had He intended Rome's meaning. Instead, He switches from direct address to the demonstrative "this."

"Arguing this in non-technical language is somewhat strained but when going from second person, "you Peter," to third person, "this

rock," then "this rock" is referring to something other than the person who is being addressed in the preceding phrase, something that we find in the immediate context.

"Sound exegesis of sacred Scripture entails thinking in paragraphs or textual units rather than prooftexting with short decontextualized passages. What is the most important idea in this Gospel narrative? If you recall from your formative years in Sunday school, when in doubt, the correct Sunday school answer was nearly always "Jesus." Indeed, Jesus is the answer here as well. The misappropriated response to Peter is praise from Jesus for Peter's inspired confession: **"You are the Christ, the Son of the Living God!"** *(Matthew 16:16) ... It is on this confession of Christ that the church is built. In Peter's own words, Christ is the cornerstone that the builders rejected which becomes the capstone (1 Peter 2:7). Every early Catholic theologian agreed, "On this rock, therefore, He said, which thou hast confessed. I will build My Church. For the Rock (Petra) is Christ; and on this foundation was Peter himself built."* (Augustine, "On the Gospel of John" Tractate 12435, as quoted in James R. White, "Answers to Catholic Claims: a Discussion of Biblical Authority" Southbridge, MA, Crowne Pubns, 1990, p 106)

What about the Fish?

The Roman Catholic Church early on dubbed the Greek IEsous (IEsous), the English Jesus, "our Fish," symbolizing his salvation by the fish, thus associating him with the Greek god Bacchus, who was called "Ichthus," the Fish, and the Egyptian sun deity Osiris. The fish became the Greek symbol for their counterfeit sun god. Dagon, the Philistine god, is also the "fish god." The Roman Catholic Church still honors Dagon in the outfitting of the Pope and bishops, as well as the eating of fish on Friday. I wonder how many Catholics realize their honoring of Dagon and other pagan deities?

This is significant in view of the frequent references such as "the eye of Horus," and the "eye of Amen-Ra," the sun god. As the locusts darkened the sun's light, the "eye of the earth" was darkened. The Egyptian version of the pagan sun god, Amen-Ra, was discredited. It is interesting to note that Amen-Ra is dressed in the same hat and cloak that the Roman Catholic Pope wears, holds the same staff that the Pope carries, and that his garments are covered totally with the ancient fertility symbol of the Tau cross. (The Tau cross symbol also stands for the name of the first sun god - Tammuz).

Present day Lucifer worship (in its many forms in many world organizations), New Age belief, Mother Earth worship, and the many interconnected groups, honor the sun god, and the gods of the stars and planets, under different names. The ancient cults of Babylon and Egypt have resurfaced and the sun god is openly worshipped as the supreme god on this earth by neo-pagans. The cults of the gods, like Isis, have resurfaced, and are now being practiced openly.

From the time of Nimrod, every culture has had its sun god worship, with the gods having different names, and with somewhat different practices. The Roman Emperor Constantine, creator of the Roman Catholic Church, changed the day of Yahweh's worship, Shabbat/Sabbath, to the day of the sun god (Sunday), making it mandatory to worship only on Sunday, and punishable by death if anyone worshipped Yahweh on the Sabbath. He worshipped the Persian sun god Mithras, whom he called *"Sol Invictus" - the "unconquerable sun."*

The Roman Catholic "monstrance," which sits on their altar, is the ancient sun god pictured with its rays extending out from a circle-centre. In the circle-centre of the monstrance is a consecrated communion wafer, supposed to be the actual body of Jesus. Jesus is worshipped on their altar, symbolically as a sun god, because Constantine elevated him to being Rome's official new sun god.

One disturbing quote I came across says, *"The priest has the power of the keys, or the power of delivering sinners from hell, of making them worthy of Paradise, and of changing them from the slaves of Satan into the children of God. And God Himself is obliged to abide by the judgment of His priests, and either not to pardon or to pardon. Were the Redeemer (Jesus) to descend into a church, and sit in a confessional to administer the sacrament of penance, and a priest to sit in another confessional, Jesus would say over each penitent, "Ego te absolve," the priest would likewise say over each of his penitent "Ego te absolve," and the penitents of each would be equally absolved... Let the priest approach the altar as another Christ."* So wrote Saint Laurence Justinian. Claiming equality with The Lord Jesus Christ is blasphemy!

It would be helpful if we now check out the official Roman Catholic doctrine on a number of key issues, and compare them with Scripture - God's Word.

Roman Catholic Teaching	Bible Teaching
They believe that Jesus merely made the way open for **salvation.** In order to enter into that salvation, one must live in obedience to the authority of the Papacy. In addition, Jesus' provision for salvation not being complete, the Roman Catholic church offers other means to assure one's salvation. The Roman Catholic church says it alone can grant this essential blessing for full salvation. The RC Church alone is the body of Christ... Those outside the church have not the Holy Spirit. ("The Teachings of the Catholic Church" p.677)	Everyone who believes in Jesus Christ has eternal life (John 3:16). Jesus made claims of being the exclusive way to the Father, (John 10:9; Ephesians 2:18). Any organization claiming this exclusivity is seeking to replace Jesus and is also declaring Jesus a liar. According to the Bible God guarantees our salvation, (John 10:27-29; Romans 10:9-17). Going to church doesn't make you a Christian any more than going to a garage makes you a mechanic.
The RC church believe that we are saved in part by good works and that **good works are necessary for salvation**.	The Bible says we are saved by grace through faith, not works. Good works come as a result of being saved, (Romans 3:24-28; Ephesians 2:8-9). A dog barks because it is a dog, not to become one. Disciples of Jesus Christ do good works because they want to show their love to God by serving Him.
The RC church believe there are **different levels of sin**; mortal (deadly) sins in which you are in danger of losing your salvation and venial (minor) sins which are not as serious. Mankind has placed different distinctions on sin (i.e. someone caught lying is not punished as severely as a person who is a murderer).	In God's eyes, sin is sin, there is no distinction, (Romans 3:10; 3:23; Exodus 20:3-17). If you have broken one, it's as if you broke them all.
Purgatory is claimed to be a place set apart from heaven and hell where souls suffer and are purged of sin. These people are claimed to be saved after death following sufficient time and the payment of money to the church.	No Scripture supports purgatory. The Bible says there is a "Great Gulf" between Heaven and Hell, (Luke 16:19-31).

Indulgences (praying for the release of Souls in purgatory)
RC believe one way of attaining salvation from the punishment of one's sins is through indulgences, which can be purchased with money or through acts of penitence, acts of charity, or other pietistic means. The idea of indulgences is based on good works meriting God's grace. Since they believe Christ's sacrifice was insufficient for the full payment of the penalty of sin, acts of piety and gifts to the Roman Catholic church may be used as partial payment for one's sins. The adequacy of an indulgence depends upon the merit attributed to it by the Roman Catholic church.

No Scripture supports this. The Bible says we are saved by faith in the sacrifice of Jesus on the Cross, and nothing else! Once you die, it's judgment time! (Ephesians 2:8-9, Hebrews 9:27). The Bible says *"May your money perish with you, because you thought you could buy the gift of God with money... Repent of this wickedness,"* (Acts 8:20-22) *"...No man can redeem the life of another or give to God a ransom for him,"* (Psalm 48:7).

Images: "It is lawful to have images in the church and to give honor and worship unto them - Images are put in churches that they may be worshipped," (Council of Trent)

The Bible states this is wrong: *"You shall not make for yourself an idol in the form of anything in heaven above or on the earth beneath, or the waters below. You shall not bow down to them or worship them; for I am the Lord your God, am a jealous God..."* (Exodus 20:4-5). *"All who worship images are put to shame, those who boast in idols - worship Him, all you gods,"* (Psalm 97:7).

Church Tradition has equal authority with the Bible according to the Council of Trent. The RC church believes there are oral traditions and teachings by Jesus that are not mentioned in the Bible; furthermore, the Roman Catholic religion has somehow been able to get this spoken word from somewhere, we're just not told how it was done.

This means whoever sits on the papal chair in Rome is considered more authoritative than the Bible itself. (Matthew 15:3,6-7; Mark 7:5-9,13) The cry of the Reformation was **sola scriptura** – the insistence that the Bible alone is the ultimate authority for all believers. The Holy Spirit's enlightenment is a safeguard against religious tyranny. *"And why do you break the command of God for the sake of your traditions?...Thus you nullify the Word of God for the sake of your tradition."*

Rome's Anathemas: Insights into the Papal Pantheon

	(Matthew 15:3-6). *"See to it that no one takes you captive through hollow and deceptive philosophy, which depends on human tradition..."* (Colossians 2:8). The Bible curses anyone who adds or takes away from the Word of God (Revelations 22:18; Deuteronomy. 4:2; 12:32; Proverbs 30:5-6; John 10:35)
Mary is a co-mediator, Mary is 'mediatrix of all graces' and Mary intercedes on our behalf RC believe that Mary is a co-redeemer with Jesus. In 1923, Pope Pius XI sanctioned Pope Benedict XV's (1914-1922) pronouncement that Mary suffered with Christ, and that with Him, she redeemed the human race. Pope Pius XI officially designated Mary the "Queen of Heaven" and "Queen of the World."	The Bible specifically states that Jesus is the only way to get to heaven. Nowhere in the Bible does it state that Mary is a co-redeemer, (John 14:6). *"For there is one God and one mediator between God and man, the man Christ Jesus,"* (1 Timothy 2:5; see also John 16:23). Only through Jesus do we have access to the Father, (Ephesians 2:18). No Scripture even hints that Mary intercedes for us, but they do state that Jesus does. *"Christ Jesus, ... is also interceding for us,"* (Romans 8:34). *"Therefore He is able to save completely those who come to God through Him, because he always lives to intercede for them,"* (Hebrews 7:25). God speaks out very clearly against the "Queen of Heaven," (Jeremiah 7:17-19).
Praying to Mary and other spirits (dead saints) in heaven other than God Himself.	Contacting the spirits of the dead is strictly forbidden, (Isaiah 8:19-20; Deuteronomy. 18:4).
Mary is the mother of God	No Scripture supports this. Jesus never called Mary 'mother' but instead 'woman.' Mary called herself the 'handmaid of the Lord.' Mary was not in existence when God created the universe (John 1:3). God is eternal and had no mother. Mary was the mother of Jesus (Acts 1:14) and cannot now be the mother of God.

Mary is the 'immaculate conception' and Mary remained a virgin after the birth of Jesus, (these made 'doctrine' in 1950). Pope Pius IX, on the Immaculate Conception of Mary that has never been revoked, states, *"Let all the children of the Catholic Church ... continue to venerate, invoke, and pray to the most blessed Virgin Mary, mother of God, conceived without original sin."* The RC church members are commanded by an 1854 papal decree to pray to and worship Mary, who has now become the Queen of Heaven.

No Scripture supports this. Mary was a sinner. The Bible says *"for all have sinned and fallen short of the glory of God,"* (Romans 3:23). Mary brought her sin offering to the Temple like all Hebrew mothers, (Luke 2:21-24, & Leviticus 12:6-8). Mary said *"My spirit rejoices in God my Saviour,"* (Luke 1:47). Why would Mary need a savior if she didn't sin? Praying to Mary is something that is not spoken of in the Bible and would make her an equal with God, thus she has become a deity to Roman Catholics. Mary needed a savior as much as anyone else and acknowledged this in Luke 1:47. The Bible states Jesus was her first-born, (Matthew 1:25) and that Jesus had brothers and sisters, (Matthew 13:55 & Mark 6:3). After Mary and Joseph married they had at least six children of their own. These half-brothers and sisters of Jesus were named as James, Joseph (or Joses), Simon, Judas and at least two sisters, (Matthew 13:55-56), one of whom was probably named Salome, (Mark 15:40). When the queen of heaven is referred to in the Bible, she is spoken of negatively, (Jeremiah 7:17-19).

Bodily Assumption of Mary - claims Mary rose into heaven in a bodily form (this was made compulsory 'doctrine' in 1950).

No Scripture supports this. The Bible says *"No one has ever gone to heaven except the one who came from heaven - the Son of Man,"* (John 3:13). When the Bible speaks of Christ's second coming it is never with Mary, but with the angels and the saints, (Zech. 14:5; 1 Thessalonians. 14:5; Jude 14; Revelation 21:2,10).

There are **seven sacraments** (The extras were invented by Peter Lombard in 1150 AD)

No Scripture supports this. The Bible has two sacraments instituted by

Jesus Christ Himself - Baptism and Communion, (This claim is admitted by the RC church but it claims tradition and its infallible authority to have seven sacraments).

Celibacy of Priests (made compulsory in 1079 AD). Some popes during the Middle Ages had wives and even mistresses.

The Bible says it is permissible to be celibate but it is not a command. Peter and most of the Apostles were married, (1 Corinthians 9:5; 1 Timothy 3:2; Matthew 8:14; & Luke 4:38).

Confessing sins to a priest: every RC priest has claimed the power to forgive or not. Confession is necessary unto salvation (Catholic Encyclopedia p. 625)

The Bible says *"Confess your sins to one another..."* (James 5:16. The apostles never heard confessions, (Acts 10:43) or forgive sins. Only God can forgive sins, (Mark 2:5-11; 1 John 1:9; Matthew 9:6). Jesus is the only mediator we need; we do not need the pope, priests, Mary or the saints, (Matthew 6:9, 12; 1 John 1:9, 2:1; 1 Timothy 2:5). God will not be bound by the arbitrary decision of a priest whether or not to absolve someone of their sins.

Infant Baptism: the RC church believes a baby can be "born again" through baptism by sprinkling, furthermore, they believe that baptism is necessary for salvation. This miracle brings a child into the family of God.

There was no infant baptism in the Bible. The Bible says the water has no effect without belief, (Acts 8:35-37). We are all born with sin and that alone disqualifies us from getting to heaven, (Romans 3:23). The act of baptism in the Bible does not guarantee you a place in heaven or make you born again, rather it is an outward act of obedience to God after you have been saved. The penitent thief on the cross was not baptized but was saved. Water baptism is not essential to salvation, (1 Corinthians 1:13-24; 15:1-5; Romans 1:16; 10:9-14; Ephesians 2:8-9; Acts 10:43; 13:38-39; 16:31; John 3:14-18; 36, 5:24; & 1 John 5:1).

Baptism performed outside the Roman Catholic church is not valid.

No Scripture supports this. Paul was baptized by Ananias who was a layman! The baptisms performed by John the Baptist were accompanied by repentance and therefore were effective to each believer.

Transubstantiation" the RC church claim the bread and wine in eucharist/communion become the real body and blood of Jesus Christ - this was made 'doctrine' in 1215. The RC church believe it is necessary for salvation to partake in the Sacrament of the Eucharist (communion). They believe they actually eat and drink the body and blood of Christ through a process called transubstantiation, whereby a priest prays over the wafer and wine and it is supernaturally turned into Christ's body. They will quote scripture, (John 6:53-58; Matthew 26:26-28) out of context to support their viewpoint.

Jesus was alive when the Last Supper took place and by interpreting this Scripture literally instead of figuratively (symbolizing his body and blood), it creates numerous problems. Jesus referred to himself as a "door," "vine," and "rock" and these descriptions are recognized as figurative, (John 10:9, 15:5; 1 Corinthians 10:4). The Bible says *"Do this in remembrance of Me,"* when Jesus celebrated the Passover prior to Calvary. It is matzah (unleavened bread) and the third cup of four - the Cup of Redemption. *"The words I have spoken to you are spirit and they are life."* Jesus also said *"I am the Bread of Life,"* (John 6:48). 1 Corinthians 11:23-26 show the instructions for Communion by Paul the apostle. According to the RC church belief and practise, Jesus is crucified afresh everyday by priests all over the world, who are putting Him to open shame. The Bible says that Jesus was physically offered up once (died for our sins), never to be repeated again, (Hebrews 9:1-28, 10:12-18). He sits on the right hand of God and does not reappear in the Mass as blood and flesh. It is very important to note that Jesus told us to take the bread (which symbolized his body) and wine (which symbolized his blood); but He did so while He was here on earth and alive. Roman Catholicism makes Jesus and his disciples into cannibals.

At Mass, Jesus Christ is sacrificed again, thousands of times each day.

The Bible rejects this renewal of sacrifice. Jesus said *"It is finished,"* a once for all sacrifice. In Greek, "It is finished" is Tetelistai! It means, *"The debt has been paid in full!"* (See Hebrews 6:6; 9:26-28; 10:10).

RC church believe that their church is founded upon the apostle Peter, that he was the first pope, therefore **Head of the Church**. The pope needs to remember this when men are bowing to him and kissing his hand like he is worthy of worship. Furthermore, history confirms the fact that there were no popes in the early church, not even in the Roman Catholic church during the first centuries of its existence.

This is convenient confusion over Peter (Petros - a stone) and Petra - a mass of rock based on Matthew 16:18-19. Petra and Petros are two different Greek words with different meanings. The Bible always refers to Jesus as Head of the Church, and Him and God as the rock, (2 Samuel 22:32; Psalm 18:31; 57:26-27). There is no evidence Peter ever left Israel to live in Rome. He wasn't even head of the Jerusalem church. The true Church of Jesus Christ was not founded upon Peter, but upon Peter's confession of Christ's deity as recorded in Matthew 16:16: *"...You are the Christ/Messiah, the Son of the living God."* The Bible says that Jesus is the foundation of the church. (Matthew 21:42; 1 Corinthians 3:11) Peter was not the first pope, nor is there any Biblical justification whatever for such an office. Peter's own inspired testimony as to his position and ministry is given in 1 Peter 5:1-4. He then identifies himself in 2nd Peter 1:1 as *"a servant and an apostle of Jesus Christ...."* Peter was a man like you and me. When Cornelius tried to worship Peter, Peter responded, *"Stand up; I myself also am a man,"* (Acts 10:25-26).

The RC church call their head, the pope, **The Holy Father.** They also entitle him as "Vicar of Christ."

The pope is a man who takes upon himself honor which belongs to no human being but to God alone. Even the very name by which he allows himself to be called (Holy Father) is highly presumptuous and blasphemous, (John 17:11). Vicar means "one who replaces."

This title of the pope pretends to replace Jesus, that is presumption of the highest deception.

The Prophet Isaiah said, **"If they do not speak according to this Word, it is because they have no light in them," (Isaiah 8:20)**

"All scripture is given by inspiration of God, and is profitable for doctrine, for reproof, for correction, for instruction in righteousness," (2 Timothy 3:16)

"Beware lest any one cheat you through philosophy and empty deceit, according to the tradition of men, according to the basic principles of the world, and not according to Christ. 9 For in him dwells all the fullness of the Godhead bodily. 10 And you are complete in Him, who is the head of all principality and power," (Colossians 2:8-10)

"Every word of God is pure: He is a shield to those who put their trust in Him. 6 Do not add to His words, lest He reprove you, and you be found a liar," (Proverbs 30:5-6)

"But even if we, or an angel from heaven, preach any other gospel to you than what we have preached to you, let him be accursed," (Galatians 1:8)

As shown above, what I have discovered is troubling, but can be dealt with through repentance.

Evolution of deception - Time-line of Roman Catholicism

The long-held claim by Roman Catholicism that it was the only unchangeable church is not supported by church history – not even Roman Catholic history. How sad to realize that this false claim influenced so many to join or to stay in this false church, which actually is the product of centuries of changes.

Most of these changes resulted from the Roman Catholic church's yielding to heathen customs and practises that were subsequently incorporated into Roman Catholic teachings and worship. The following is a partial list of heathen, unscriptural practices that became a part of Roman Catholic dogma over a period of seventeen centuries. Some of the dates given are approximate. In many cases, these heresies were even debated for years before being given the status of required beliefs:

300 AD	Prayers for the dead
312 AD	Making the sign of the cross
375 AD	Veneration of angels and dead saints
375 AD	Use of images in worship
394 AD	The Mass as a daily celebration
431 AD	Beginning of the exaltation of Mary; the term, "Mother of God" applied at Council of Ephesus
500 AD	Priests dress differently from laymen
526 AD	Extreme Unction (Last Rites)
593 AD	Doctrine of Purgatory (Gregory 1st)
600 AD	Prayers to Mary and dead saints
709 AD	Kissing Pope's foot
786 AD	Worship of cross, images & relics
995 AD	Canonization of dead saints
1079	Celibacy of priesthood

Rosary beads with ritual prayers attached to each bead. Mary is the focus of the majority of them.

1090	The Rosary (Peter the Hermit) - borrowed from Hinduism, Buddhism & Islam
1190	Sale of Indulgences
1215	Transubstantiation (Innocent 3rd)
1215	Verbal Confession of sins to a priest, Pope Innocent 3rd, Lateran Council
1220	Adoration of the wafer - the Host. Pope Honorius
1229	Bible forbidden for lay people, Council of Toledo
1414	Cup forbidden to the people (non-priests) at communion, Council of Constance
1439	Purgatory proclaimed as a dogma
1439	The doctrine of the Seven Sacraments confirmed
1508	Jesuit Order founded
1545	Tradition declared of equal authority with Bible by Council of Trent
a.	Denied every doctrine of the Reformation, from Sola Scriptura to *"salvation by grace through faith alone,"*
b.	Pronounced 125 anathemas (eternal damnation) upon anyone believing what evangelicals believe and preach today. Here is a sampling:
1546	Apocryphal books added to Bible
1854	Immaculate Conception of Mary
1870	First Vatican Council
c.	Defined the infallibility of the pope in matters of faith and morals
d.	Confirmed Unum Sanctum (no salvation outside of the Roman Catholic Church).
1950	Assumption of the Virgin Mary (bodily ascension into heaven shortly after her death)
1965	Second Vatican Council

Second Vatican Council made no new doctrines, nor did it change or repudiate any old ones; Trent and the First Vatican Council stand as is (The Second Vatican Council verified and validated all the anathemas of Trent). The Second Vatican Council reaffirmed such Roman heresies as papal supremacy; the Roman priesthood; the mass as an unbloody sacrifice of Christ; a polluted sacramental gospel; Catholic tradition on equal par with Scripture; Mary as the Queen of Heaven and co-Redemptrix with Christ; auricular confession; Mariolatry; pilgrimages to "holy shrines;" purgatory; prayers to and for the dead; etc.

a. Mary proclaimed Mother of the Roman Catholic church.

b. Reaffirmed the infallibility of the pope (and even when he does not speak ex-cathedra, all Roman Catholics must still give complete submission of mind and will to what he says).

c. Divided Roman Catholic doctrine into that which is essential core of theology, and must be received by faith, and that which is still an undefined body of theology which Roman Catholics may question and debate without repudiating their essential core.

d. Established 20 complex rules concerning when and how any indulgence may be obtained, and condemned *"with anathema those who say that indulgences are useless or that the Church does not have the power to grant them ... [for] the task of winning salvation."*

Further Pagan Adoptions

The Zucchetti which is worn by Catholic priests, cardinals and the Pope, represents respect, fear and submission to Cybele, the Mother Goddess of Rome. The Cap of Cybele is one of the oldest and most sacred pagan religious symbols of humanity, dating back to 2,000 B.C. The skull cap was worn by the sun priests of Egypt. It is a thin, slightly rounded skullcap now commonly known by various titles including the Yarmulke (Jewish) and Kufi (Muslims). The Roman Catholic Church calls it the Zucchetti.

Vatican Hill was the site of the largest ancient temple to Cybele. Ashtoreth the goddess of fertility, sexuality and war, was known as Cybele in Rome.

The Bible warns against worshiping her, **"Then the children of Israel again did evil in the sight of the LORD, and served the Baals and the Ashtoreths,"** Judges 10:6.

The Bible declares **"For a man indeed ought not to cover his head, since he is the image and glory of God,"** 1 Corinthians 11:7.

Ask yourself, why do Roman Catholic priests, Bishops and the Pope, wear the Cap of Cybele?

The Mitre hat that is worn by Roman Catholic priests, cardinals and the Pope, (and Anglican/ Episcopal and some other bishops) represents Dagon the Babylonian fish god. The ancient Babylonians worshiped Dagon, the god of agriculture, plenty (food) and good fortune. The Babylonian priests wore a headdress that represented the worship of Cybele and Dagon. It featured an open-fish mouth on the head, with the rest of the fish body forming a cloak.

In the Roman Empire, it was worn by the head priest of Cybele (the Magna Mater) or the Great Queen Mother Goddess. Today the Roman Catholic Cardinals, Bishops and the Pope all wear the open fish-mouth mitre, which represents the worship of Cybele and Dagon. The Mitre hat of Dagon is always worn over the Kippa of Ashtoreth/Cybele, as you can see in the picture of Pope Francis.

God warned the Jews not to worship the gods of Babylon, **"I will utter My judgments against them concerning all their wickedness, because they have forsaken Me and have burned incense to other gods, and worshipped the works of their own hands," Jeremiah 1:16.**

Ask yourself, why do Roman Catholic Cardinals, Bishops and the Pope, all wear the mitre of Dagon?

The Obelisk in St. Peter's Square represents the worship of the Sun god. Obelisks were prominent in the architecture of the ancient Egyptians, who placed them at the entrance of a temple, marking it as a zone of sun worship. They represent the Sun God Ra, the Egyptians' greatest deity; the creator of humanity, the source of all heat and light, the being on which man was totally dependent. The most well-known Egyptian obelisk was re-erected in 1586 A.D., in front of St. Peter's Basilica. It is surrounded by a sun wheel, with the points lining up with the Vernal Equinox, the Summer Solstice and the Winter Solstice.

During the sunrise on the Vernal Equinox, the sun causes the obelisk to cast its shadow onto the dome of St. Peter's Basilica, which represents the sexual union of the sun god and moon goddess. Another Egyptian obelisk sits in front of the Pantheon of ancient Rome, which housed statues of their pagan gods. The obelisk was originally constructed by Pharaoh Ramses 2nd for the Temple of Ra in Heliopolis. It was brought to Rome in ancient times where it was used near a shrine to the Egyptian god Isis. The Pantheon was dedicated to 'pan theos,' meaning "all the gods." When it became a Roman Catholic Church, it was dedicated to the Virgin Mary and all the martyrs.

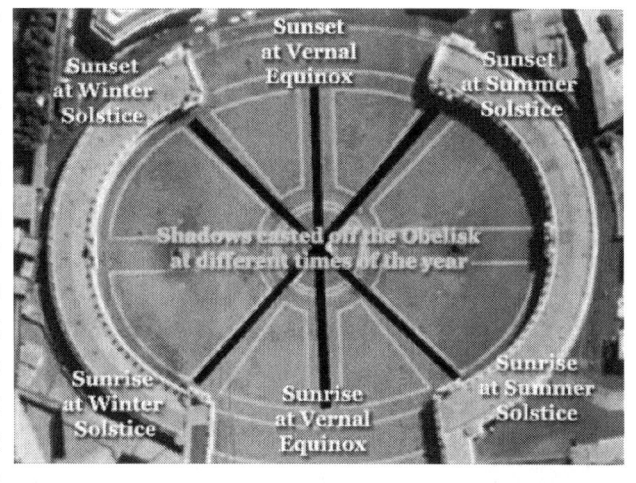

God's 2nd commandment says, **"You shall not make for yourself any carved image, or any likeness of anything that is in heaven above, or that is in the earth beneath, or that is in the water under the earth; you shall not bow down to them nor serve them. For I, the Lord your God, am a jealous God," Exodus 20:4-5.**

Ask yourself, why does the Roman Catholic Church venerate pagan monuments to the Sun god?

The six-sided star is the supreme symbol of Satanic tyranny. The hexagram has been used by people such as the pagan Babylonians, Egyptians and Assyrians, to directly or indirectly worship Satan. Helena Blavatsky wrote that *"Lucifer is the true God,"* and she incorporated the hexagram in the emblem of the Theosophical Society, which she founded in 1875. Satanists, Luciferians, astrologers and witches use it to invoke the power of demons. The six-sided star numerically equals 666 (6 points, 6 triangles, 6-sided hexagon).

Christians pass it off as the 'Star of David' but the truth is that King David never used a star, so calling it a nice sounding name hides what it really represents. King Solomon used it in witchcraft, magic and idolatrous worship to Ashtoreth and to Moloch. Stephen accused the Jewish leaders, **"And you took up the tabernacle of Moloch, and the star of your god Remphan, the images you made to worship them," Acts 7:43.**

Ask yourself, why does the Roman Catholic Church use the Satanic six-sided star?

The eight-pointed star represents the pagan goddess Ishtar, the light bringer. In Babylonian symbolism, the goddess Ishtar is represented by an eight-pointed star burst, and she is associated with the planet of Venus. Ishtar was the Babylonian High-Mother-Goddess, the goddess of fertility, love and war. Her cult was the most important one in ancient Babylon. An eight-point star enclosed within a circle is the symbol for the sun god, as it's points represent the solstices and equinoxes. The *"Babylonian star-cult is the core and the archetype of subsequent astrology."* At the centre of St. Peter's Basilica, the Pope sits in the middle of eight 8-sided stars.

Ask yourself, why does the Roman Catholic Church use the eight-pointed star of Ishtar?

The Maltese Cross represents Shamash, the god of the Sun and Justice. In the image, an ancient Assyrian king is wearing a cross on his chest, just like the one seen on the Pope's robe. Shamash (Akkadian Šamaš = "Sun"), was a native Mesopotamian deity and the sun god in the Akkadian, Assyrian and Babylonian pantheons. Shamash was the god of justice in Babylonia and Assyria, corresponding to Sumerian Utu. This cross was identified with a Sun god eight centuries before Christ and long before it was called the Maltese Cross by the Knights of Malta. It's also called the Iron Cross. Roman Catholic Adolph Hitler renewed use of the Iron Cross in 1939 and superimposed the Nazi swastika in its centre.

Ask yourself, why does the Pope wear the cross of Shamash the Sun god?

Pine cones symbolize the worship of the solar god Osiris. Pine cones are associated with spiritual enlightenment by ancient Babylonians, Egyptians and Greeks. They represent the mysterious link between the physical and the spiritual worlds, which can be found in the human brain, in the pineal gland. The pine cone staff is a symbol of the solar god Osiris and originated in Egypt where he was their messiah who died for his people and whose Mother, Isis, was worshiped as the Virgin Mother. The Vatican also has the world's largest pine cone that once decorated a fountain in ancient Rome next to a vast Temple of Isis. At the Old St. Peter's Basilica, it was dedicated to Attis, son and lover of Cybele. The Catholic Church then relocated it to what's now called the Vatican Court of the Pigna.

Egyptian God Osiris Staff

Pine Cone On Pope Staff

Ask yourself, why do Popes use pine cones which symbolize the solar god Osiris?

The Popes of Rome are Sun Worshipers. In the middle of St. Peter's Square is an ancient Egyptian obelisk, which represents the Sun god Ra of Egypt. It was placed in the middle of a giant Sun wheel, which is lined up with the solar solstices and equinoxes. When an obelisk is placed in front of a temple, it designates it as a place of Sun worship. The Egyptian obelisk sits directly in front of St. Peter's Basilica, designating it as a temple of Sun worship. The pagans believe that their Sun god is conceived on 21st March, the (northern) Spring Equinox. You can see this played out annually at the Vatican, when the rising Sun causes the shadow of the Egyptian obelisk (which is a phallic symbol representing Nimrod, the Sun god) to fall onto the dome of St. Peter's Basilica (symbolizing the womb of the moon goddess Semiramis), representing their annual sexual union.

Nine months later their son Tammuz is born. The cross on top of the obelisk actually is the letter 't' which represents the sun god Tammuz. The pagans believe that on the northern Winter solstice, 21st December, that the Sun god dies, as the Sun is at its furthest point away from the earth; that it is dead for three days, and then is reborn, so they celebrate his re-birth on 25th December. Tammuz, who was symbolically conceived at the Vatican on 21st March, is the reincarnation of the Sun god Nimrod. His birthday is celebrated on Christ-mass.

Note: The Messiah of the Bible was conceived in December, on Hanukkah (the festival of lights, as He is the light of the world); and He was born in the fall,/autumn on the Feast of Tabernacles. Christ-mass symbolically represents the birth of the Roman Sun god *Sol Invictus*; which points back to the Babylonian sun god Tammuz.

St. Peter's Basilica has a huge sun symbol behind the stage where the Pope sits.

The Basilica of St. Mary and the Martyrs, used to be the Roman Pantheon which housed their pagan gods. It too has an Egyptian obelisk in front of it, designating it as a temple of Sun worship. The Catholic Mass is performed in a place that was built to worship all pagan gods.

The Eucharist host wafer is round, representing the Sun god. They hold it up to revere it. Then they place it on a crescent moon (representing the female womb of the moon goddess), which represents their symbolic sexual union. This symbolically makes the wafer the flesh of their Sun god Tammuz. This is carried out every day, thousands of times a day throughout the world. The Eucharist wafer has a 't' on it, which represents their Sun god Tammuz. On Ash Wednesday, they mark the foreheads of Roman Catholics with a t for Tammuz. The 40 days of Lent symbolizes the 40 years that Tammuz lived. Lent ends with Easter when it is tradition to eat ham. This symbolizes the remembrance of Tammuz, who was killed by a wild boar. The top leaders of the Roman Catholic Church worship the Sun god of Babylon, which is ultimately Satan worship. They fulfil the prophecy of Mystery, Babylon the Great; as they worship the pagan gods of Babylon, under the guise of Christianity. And they cause innocent Roman Catholics to unknowingly partake in these pagan rituals.

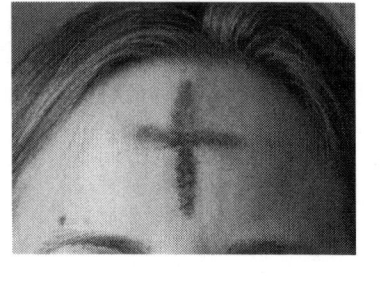

In Revelation 18:4 Messiah Jesus/Yeshua told people to come of out the apostate church before it's too late. **"Come out of her, my people, lest you share in her sins, and lest you receive of her plagues."**

I encourage you to worship the true Messiah of Scriptures, not the false one that was created by the Popes of Rome.

The 95 Theses of Luther

Choices must be made

"It is necessary to salvation that every man should submit to the Pope," (so stated Pope Boniface 8th Unum Sanctum, 1303 AD.)

"For by grace you have been saved through faith; and that not of yourselves: it is the gift of God, not of works, lest anyone should boast," Ephesians 2:8, 9.

Here lie two totally contradictory statements. They cannot both be correct. The one that you believe will depend on which authority you accept - Holy Scripture from God; or a religious organization that gets so much else wrong?

The Roman Catholic Church has long been antagonistic to the doctrine of salvation by grace. If salvation is by grace, who needs "mass?" If salvation is by grace, who needs to fear purgatory? If Jesus Christ is our mediator, who needs the Pope or his priests? If the Pope cannot intimidate people into obeying him, how can he force a nation to obey him?

The Holy Bible is the arch-enemy of the Roman Catholic Church. Rome can only rule over ignorant, fear-filled people. The Holy Bible turns "unlearned and ignorant" men into gospel preachers and casts out "all fear."

Rome had to find a way to supplant the true gospel with "another gospel." The only way to do this is to eliminate our faith in the Word of God.

A major blow to the authority of Rome came in 1517, when a young Catholic priest by the name of Martin Luther nailed his historic 95 theses on the church door in the town of Wittenburg, Germany.

The nail drove deep into the hearts of truly born-

Martin Luther

again Christians who had for centuries been laboring under the tyranny of the Roman Catholic Church.

The people flocked to their new, brave leader. From this, Lutheranism was established, but even more important, the fires of the Reformation were kindled.

In 1545 the Roman Catholic Church formed the Council of Trent. This Council of Trent systematically denied the teachings of the Reformation. The Council decreed that "tradition" was of equal authority with the Bible. It decreed also that justification was not by faith alone in the shed blood of Jesus Christ. In fact, it stated that anyone believing in this vital Bible doctrine was cursed.

The Council's exact words are: *"If anyone saith that justifying faith is nothing else but confidence in the divine mercy which remits sins for Christ's sake or that this confidence alone is that whereby we are justified, let him be* **anathema.***"*

We now see that the Roman Catholic Church is guilty of officially cursing Jesus Christ!

Would God use this church to preserve His Words?

Men have long been worshippers of education. If an educator makes a claim, the "common" people will follow, because they have convinced themselves that anyone with that much education can't be wrong.

Evolution has been accepted as a fact by the average Westerner because educators claim that it is true. The fact that they can produce no evidence to substantiate their theory is incidental. Education says it is so!

The Jesuits' task was to entice Protestant scholarship back to Rome. (Note: The Jesuits are a Military Religious Order of the Roman Catholic Church. The Jesuit Oath includes: *"IUSTUM, NECAR, REGES, IMPIOUS,"* The meaning of which is: *"It is just to exterminate or annihilate impious or heretical Kings, Governments, or Rulers...")*

The Jesuits knew that they could not wean the leaders of Protestantism back into Rome as long as the stubborn "heretics" clung to the Scripture text of the Reformers. This Bible would have to be replaced with one which contained the pro-Roman Catholic readings of Jerome's Vulgate and the Jesuit translation of 1582. It would be necessary to "educate" the Protestant scholars to believe that their Reformation Text was unreliable and that their Authorised Version was "not scholarly." Once thus programmed, the egotistical scholars would spontaneously attack their own Bible and believe that they were helping God.

Jesuit Superior General Adolfo Nicolas Pachon, (also known as the Black Pope), & right, Pope Francis

The most important objective to be realized would be to replace the Bible as the final authority.

At the time, the Authorised Version of the Bible had become a mightier foe than Rome had anticipated as Dr. McClure points out: *"The printing of the English Bible has proved to be by far the mightiest barrier ever reared to repel the advance of Popery, and to damage all the resources of the Papacy. Originally intended for the five or six millions who dwelt within the narrow limits of the British Islands, it at once formed and fixed their language, till then unsettled; and has since gone with that language to the isles and shores of every sea."*

The Roman Catholic Church has been built on about 20% twisted Scripture and 80% superstition. Where men were ignorant, it could rule by playing on their fears. But, when the "ignorant and unlearned" people received Christ as personal Savior and clung faithfully to the Holy Bible, they were not only immovable but could easily refute any heresy, be it Catholic or otherwise.

Deception Avoidable

All of the deception and false doctrine would have been avoidable had the church leaders measured their beliefs with God's Word, the Bible.

It all comes back to one decision - do you choose to believe the Bible or not? God says the following about His Word:

"All Scripture is God-breathed and is useful for teaching, rebuking, correcting and training in righteousness," 2 Timothy 3:16.

Let me provide two quotations that will also help:

"The errors (of translation) affect no more than one-one thousandth part of the Biblical text, so we believe them far too insignificant to shake our faith in the inerrancy of the original manuscripts," said Dr. René Pache, of Lausanne University, and Principal of the Emmaus Bible College.

"Both the authenticity and the general integrity of the books of the New Testament may be regarded as finally established." Sir Frederick Kenyon, Director & Principal Librarian - British Museum. (quoted by Nicky Gumbel, "Questions of Life p. 25)

These expert scholars are saying we can believe the Bible. We don't question the historic record of men such as Herodotus, Thucydides, Tacitus, the record of Caesar's Gallic Wars or Livy. Check out the following:

New Testament Reliability

Work	When Written	Earliest copy	Time span years	No. of Copies
Herodotus	488-428BC	900AD	1300	8
Thucydides	460-400BC	900AD	1300	8
Tacitus	100AD	1100AD	1000	20
Caesar's Gallic Wars	58-50BC	900AD	950	9
Livy's Roman History	59BC-17AD	900AD	900	20
New Testament script)	40-100AD	130AD	300	5366 (Greek) 350 (full manu- 10,000(Latin) 9,300 others

The bottom line is that we can trust God's Word, the Holy Bible, and we must use it to measure our lives, beliefs, doctrines and church practices.

Those whose choice is to reject the Bible and all it contains, despite the overwhelming evidence of its reliability, have consequences to face some time in the future, maybe sooner than they think.

Examples of false teaching affecting Christians Today

Pope Francis Says Having A Personal Relationship With Jesus Is Dangerous And Harmful

Pope Francis, in June 2016, says that the "only way" to connect with God is through the (Roman Catholic) church. And that a personal relationship with Jesus is wrong.

Here is what Pope Francis said:
"There is no "do-it-yourself" in the church, no "free-lancers." How many times did we hear Pope Benedict describe the church as a "we" church? Sometime you may hear someone say, "I believe in God, in Jesus, but the church... I don't care." How many times have we heard this? This is wrong. There are those who believe you can have a personal, direct and immediate relationship with Jesus Christ outside the communion and mediation of the church. These temptations are dangerous and harmful. They are, in the words of the great Pope Paul VI, "absurd dichotomies." It's true that journeying together is challenging, and sometimes it can be tiring: it may be that some brother or sister (in the church) makes us face a problem, or scandalizes us. But the Lord entrusted his message of salvation to humans, all of us, as witnesses; and in our brothers and sisters, with their gifts and limits, who come to us and make themselves known. This means belonging to the (RC) church..."

This is incorrect. To have a personal relationship with Jesus wherever you are is Bible Scripture truth!

"Jesus said to him, I am the way, the truth, and the life: no man comes to the Father, but by me," (John 14:6).

As Disciples of Jesus Christ, we know that our faith must have a factual basis to it. The standard for faith, for our understanding of God, and how to live our lives in service to Him, must come from Scripture

Pope Francis having discussion & meal with "Protestant" leaders, including Kenneth Copeland

– God-breathed and Holy Spirit inspired, (see 2 Timothy 3:16). When the Church of Rome states categorically that tradition is equal and even superior to the Bible's clear teaching, we must **not only dispute but also reject** that view. There can be no common ground. God gives everyone free will. We come to faith in Him through Jesus Christ freely – not under compulsion. The reason is simple – compulsion makes spiritual robots, and the like. Freedom of thought and understanding, with a solid Biblical foundation, brings a sense of love and devotion that is willing to serve from a regenerated heart and a cleansed spirit.

We reject the concepts from the religion of Islam because you have a choice to convert to them or die. 103 surah's or verses of the Qur'an say it's okay to take your head off if you won't convert to Islam. The followers of Islam have killed about 300,000 Christians each year for the past 25 years running. There have been major massacres of Christians and others every century since Mohammed in the 6th & 7th centuries.

Pope Gregory 13th struck a medal to celebrate the St. Bartholomew's Day massacre.

But let's not forget that the Roman Catholic Church has done similar to anyone who wouldn't convert to their views. What about the 30,000 Protestant/ Huguenots murdered by Roman Catholics on St. Bartholomew's Day (23-24 August, 1547) in

Paris France. (That's the same year the Canon on Sacraments was promulgated from the Council of Trent.) Or what about the report from Canon Llorente, Secretary to the Inquisition in Madrid Spain, that between 1790 and 1792 some three million non-Catholics were condemned, with 300,000 burned at the stake. *"Do not forget that the Church has never officially admitted that these practices were evil, nor apologized to the world or to any of the victims or their descendants. Nor could Pope John Paul 2nd apologize today because "the doctrines responsible for those terrible things still underpins his position."* Dave Hunt quoted from the Berean Call, July 1994 (page 265, "Protestants & Catholics, Do They Now Agree?" by Dr. John Ankerberg & Dr. John Weldon.)

Pope Benedict 16th in 2007 with Andrew Bertie, Grand Master of the Order of Malta - the Catholic/Masonic order

We could also check Fox's Book of Martyrs of the British Christians burned at the stake by Roman Catholic authorities because they wouldn't accept the false doctrines of the Roman church such as mass.

Even now in Mexico and other Latin American nations where Roman Catholicism has been predominant for centuries, many Christians are persecuted, including expulsion from their homes, beaten up and killed on instructions from local Catholic priests and bishops. The good news is that there are now more people attending Evangelical and Pentecostal churches in Latin America than go to Catholic mass any more. People in increasing numbers are seeking freedom and reality, not religion and control.

Pope John Paul 2nd with the Anti-Christ throne with the Satanic/Black Mass cross.

Pope John Paul 2nd with the idol of the Queen of Heaven

Pope John Paul 2nd Says "There is no hell!"

When Pope John Paul 2nd stated in 1999 that there is no real place called "hell," he effectively called Jesus a liar. In Luke chapter 16, Jesus explains about heaven and hell with a significant amount of details. In fact, we learn more about hell from the lips of Jesus through the New Testament than from any other reliable source. While it may explain the desperate need for Biblical correction of Roman Catholic doctrine, to reject the clear teaching of Jesus is apostasy and cannot be otherwise explained!

Statement from Pope John Paul 2nd published in The Globe & Mail, Toronto Canada, 29 July, 1999

THE ULTIMATE PUNISHMENT

Throwing cold water on the fires of hell

Pope says hell isn't 'a physical place,' raising some tricky issues

Jesus tells us about hell in 238 verses in the Bible. Jesus believes Hell is an actual place in Matthew 25:46; that it's a place of physical suffering in Matthew 22:13 & Luke 16:24; and an irrevocable destination in Luke 16:26

Further Examples of false teaching affecting Christians Today

During The Reformation, (1517-1685) most of the reformers well understood that the prophecy of the Anti-Christ referred to the massive system of Roman Catholicism that developed during the Middle Ages. Of course, Rome did not appreciate this interpretation. What follows is Rome's course of action to abolish this understanding.

Toward the end of the Reformation, two learned scholars began, by different means, to accomplish the same end: To deflect all thinking away from identifying the Anti-Christ with the Papal system.

These were Jesuit theologians Luis del Alcázar (1554–1613) a Spanish Jesuit promoted 'Preterism.' His view was that everything in the Apocalypse/Revelation, except the three final chapters had already occurred.

Alcazar devoted himself to bring into prominence this **Preterist** view. He did so to prove that the prophecies of Anti-Christ were fulfilled before the popes ever ruled in Rome, and therefore could not possibly apply to the Papacy. He is known for his *Vestigatio Arcani Sensus in Apocalypsi* published in 1614 after his death, in which the preterist method of interpretation was set forth.

Next was the Jesuit Francisco Ribera, who about 1580 brought about *'The Futurist System.'* This claims that all the prophecies refer to some future supernatural individual who is yet to appear.

Fast Forward Two Hundred Years. The next Jesuit was Manuel De Lacunza (1731–1801) a Jesuit from Chile. He wrote his manuscript *La Venida del Mesías en Gloria y Magestad* - *"The Coming of the Messiah in Glory and Majesty,"* under the pen name of Juan Josafat Rabbi Ben-Ezra about 1791.

Lacunza wrote under an assumed Jewish name to obscure the fact that he was a Roman Catholic and to give his book greater approval among Protestants, his intended audience. He also taught **Futurism**, proposing that the Anti-Christ was still off in the future, deliberately trying to take the pressure off the Papacy. His manuscript was published in London, Spain, Mexico and Paris between 1811 and 1826.

The whole theory of the secret rapture with its future Anti-Christ had its origin with the Jesuits in an attempt to take the blame off the Papacy.

Along came Edward Irving (1792-1834) a Scottish Presbyterian and forerunner of the Pentecostal and Charismatic movements, translated Lacunza's work from Spanish into English. This was published in London in 1827 by L.B. Seeley & Sons, it included Irving's own lengthy preface.

This was followed by John Nelson Darby, (1800-1882), a Brethren preacher and writer of the time in England - who was largely responsible for introducing the teaching of a secret rapture on a large scale.

The teaching spread to the United States in the 1850s and 1860s, where it was to receive its biggest boost when Cyrus I. Scofield, a strong believer in Darby's teachings, incorporated it into the notes of his Scofield Reference Bible, published in 1909.

This Bible was promoted by Oxford University Press. It is basically a King James Version but with extensive footnote commentaries by Cyrus Scofield and consulting editors. In every passage that could possibly be related to end-times, the pre-trib rapture doctrine is espoused.

Many readers throughout the years have been unaware of the difference between words of Scripture and the opinions of Scofield. This version of the Bible has been so promoted that its views have affected every church and town in America and much of the Western world.

One example will suffice - The Parable of the Weeds in Matthew chapter 13.

24 He put another parable before them, saying, "The kingdom of heaven may be compared to a man who sowed good seed in his field, but while his men were sleeping, his enemy came and sowed weeds[among the wheat and went away. So when the plants came up and bore grain, then the weeds appeared also. And the servants of the master of the house came and said to him, 'Master, did you not sow good seed in your field? How then does it have weeds?' He said to them, 'An enemy has done this.' So the servants said to him, 'Then do you want us to go and gather them?' But he said, 'No, lest in gathering the weeds you root up the wheat along with them. 30 Let both grow together until the harvest, and at harvest time I will tell

the reapers, **Gather the weeds first** and bind them in bundles to be burned, but gather the wheat into my barn," (Matthew 13:24-30) The Scofield Reference Bible says: *"At the end of this age the tares are set apart for burning, but **first the wheat** is gathered into the barn."*

Wheat

The Scofield Bible Notes say the exact OPPOSITE of what the Scripture actually says in Matthew 13:30.

Significant Pre-Trib Rapture teachers who have promoted this false teaching that originated with the Jesuits include:

Tares

The Moody Bible Institute acquire *(the Assemblies of God went to Moody to Sunday School materials.)*

Dallas Theological Seminary
Hal Lindsay -Late Great Planet Earth
Tim LaHaye –Left Behind series
Jack Van Impe
Chuck Missler
John Hagee
Perry Stone
John Ankerberg

Bob Jones University
J. Vernon McGee
Grant Jeffrey
Dave Hunt
David Wilkerson
David Reagan
Jimmy DeYoung
Jonathan Cahn

Influential Pre-Tribulation Teachers

The Timing of the Rapture is not a Salvation Issue - it is NOT a reason for disciples of the Lord Jesus Christ to ever break fellowship with any other Brother or Sister.

Rome's Anathemas: Insights into the Papal Pantheon - 75

But it is a GLORY ISSUE!

"Seventy weeks are determined for your people and for your holy city, to finish the transgression, to make an end of sins, to make reconciliation for iniquity, to bring in everlasting righteousness, to seal up vision and prophecy, and to anoint the Most Holy," (Daniel 9:24).

The real tragedy of the rapture theory is that it takes the beautiful verses of Daniel 9:24, including the Coming of Jesus, His Baptism, His Finished Work on the Cross, **and then wrongly applies them to Anti-Christ**.

Daniel states that it is Jesus who caused the sacrificial system of the Jews to cease when He died on the Cross. Saying that it is the Anti-Christ that causes the sacrifice and oblation to cease after three and one-half years confuses something Messiah Yeshua/Jesus Christ has done, and applies it to the devil instead. Surely this is a heresy!

For those Followers of Messiah Yeshua/Jesus Christ for whom His Glory is an ultimate issue, this misinterpretation is tragic and infuriating.

"Behold He is coming with clouds and every eye will see Him," (Revelation 1:7).

This is a stark example of how Roman Catholic apologists have influenced non-Catholic teaching in a detrimental way.

What about Infant Baptism?

Some Christian denominations practice "infant" or baby baptism, usually by 'sprinkling' with a few drops of water. This is sometimes called 'Christening.' In the Orthodox (Greek and Russian etc.) Churches, infants are baptized by immersion up to their neck.

During the Dark Ages (when the Roman church had adopted paganism and Anti-Semitism as a life-style, and thereby devalued itself by becoming a political organization instead of being life-changing through the Holy Spirit), a particular problem arose. People practising witchcraft got the weird notion that if they sacrificed a person who hadn't been "baptized," that person would go to hell rather than heaven. Children were at obvious risk. (This concept has no Biblical basis to it, of course.) The Bishop of Rome at the time simply declared that baptizing infants would overcome this dilemma, which it largely did.

In a council of the Church held at Ravenna in 1311, Pope Clement 5th declared that, *"It is a matter of indifference whether immersion or sprinkling is used."*

One of the ablest Roman Catholic theologian, Rev. S.J. Hunter, SJ, remarks, *"It is impossible for infant baptism to be discussed directly between a Catholic and a Baptist. They have no common ground. The Baptist urges that the Scriptures everywhere teach faith as a prerequisite to baptism. The Catholic defends his practice as to infants by the authority of the (Roman Catholic) Church, which the Baptist refuses to recognize."* ("Outlines of Dogmatic Theology," Vol.3, page 222).

Rev. Hunter goes on to say, *"The great bulk of Protestant sects employ infant baptism. Yet there is no trace in Scripture of Christian baptism being administered to anyone who was not capable of asking for it.* **The practice of infant baptism, therefore, cannot be defended on Scriptural grounds**.*"* (Vol.1, page 148). *(Emphasis added)*

"The change from the ordinary rite – from immersion to sprinkling

– was made by the authority of the (Roman Catholic) Church, which is sufficient." (page 216).

The Roman Catholic Church has consistently claimed that the official teaching of their Church is equal in authority with the Bible. The Reformation, started by Martin Luther and others, was the result of those who chose to believe the authority of the Bible above all other authority. This is what Rev. Hunter is commenting on above. Roman Catholics practise infant sprinkling because their church says they can, and they make no pretence to obey Scripture.

Other Christian denominations that practice infant sprinkling cannot claim the authority of the Bible for their practice of sprinkling infants, as Rev. Hunter points out. There is no apparent reason for this practise other than that Pope Clement said they could do it that way.

The 'baptism' of babies gives a false sense of spiritual security to its recipients, who are often strangely resistant to later appeals, as if inoculated against the gospel. It was Martin Luther who termed infant baptism as **"Unbeliever's Baptism."**

Fundamentally, "Christening" or "infant baptism" is the dedication of a child to God (or to that church denomination) with water. As such, it fails the Biblical standard of baptism that requires a person to be old enough to believe in Jesus Christ and who personally accepts and affirms what Jesus did on Calvary's cross for them.

Confirmation by an authority such as a bishop in later life is a poor substitute for the Biblical model. Recipients of 'Christening' or infant sprinkling need to be informed that they have not yet received Christian Baptism. When they come to faith in Jesus Christ they still need to obey the Biblical command to be baptized.

What about The Sabbath?

The Bible Sabbath is very important - for it is the very centre of our worship of God. If men were later to try to change it to another day, we would surely expect a Bible prophecy saying that it would happen. And that's exactly what happened.

"And he shall speak words against the Most High (God), and shall wear out the saints of the Most High, and think to change the time (of sacred feasts and holy days) and the law; and the saints shall be given into his hand for a time, two times and half a time (three and a half years)," (Daniel 7:25 AMP.)

After the New Testament was finished and the original Apostles had died, men tried to transfer the sacredness from the seventh day to the first day of the week to honour the sun god of Constantine. They tried to change the "time law."

Following are some quotes to confirm this:

"It is well to remind the Presbyterians, Baptists, Methodists, and all other Christians, that the Bible does not support them anywhere in their observance of Sunday. Sunday is an institution of the Roman Catholic Church, and those who observe the day observe a commandment of the Catholic Church." (Priest Brady, in an address at Elizabeth, New Jersey, March 17th, 1903, reported in the Elizabeth NJ News of March 18th, 1903.)

"You may search the Bible from Genesis to Revelation, and you will not find a single line authorizing the sanctification of Sunday. The Scriptures enforce the religious observance of Saturday, a day which we never sanctify." (James Cardinal Gibbon, "The Faith of our Fathers," chapter 8)

"If Protestants would follow their Bible, they would worship God on the Sabbath day. In keeping the Sunday they are following the law of the Catholic Church." (Albert Smith, Chancellor of the Archdiocese of Baltimore, replying for the Cardinal, in a letter of February 10th, 1920.)

"We hold upon this earth the place of God Almighty." (Pope Leo 13th, Encyclical Letter, June 20th, 1894; The Great Encyclical Letters of Leo 13th, p. 304.)

"Prove to me from the Bible alone that I am bound to keep Sunday holy. There is no such law in the Bible. It is the law of the holy Catholic Church alone. The Bible says, "Remember the Sabbath day to keep it holy." The Catholic Church says, No! By my divine power I abolish the Sabbath day and command you to keep holy the first day of the week. And lo! The entire civilized world bows down in reverent obedience to the command of the Holy Catholic Church." (Priest Thomas Enright, CSSR, President of the Redemptorist College, Kansas MO. in a lecture at Hartford, Kansas Weekly Call, February 22, 1884, and the American Sentinel, a New York Roman Catholic journal, in June 1893, p. 173.)

"Of course the Catholic Church claims that the change (of the time law) was her act... and the act is a mark of her ecclesiastical power." (From the office of Cardinal Gibbons, through chancellor H.F.Thomas, November 11, 1895.)

Pope Francis with the idol of the Queen of Heaven

Idolatry parade in Guatemala for the Queen of Heaven

Saints and Dead People

While I am completing this book, the media are reporting the elevation of Mother Theresa of Calcutta to Sainthood in the Roman Catholic Church. The promotion was declared publicly by Pope Francis on the basis that two different people had been healed of significant illnesses after praying to Theresa, who died in 1997. After authenticating these healings, the Vatican proclaims the status of "Saint" on the person to whom prayers were aimed. This proclamation becomes compulsory belief for all Roman Catholics, although it has no Biblical basis whatsoever.

Let's look at what the term "saint" actually means. Vines Expository Dictionary describes saints as a term ... *"not applied merely to persons of exceptional holiness or to those, who having died, were characterized by exceptional acts of saintliness. ...See especially 2 Thess. 1:10 where "His saints" are also described as "them that believed," i.e. the whole number of the redeemed."*

One of the world's best Bible teachers, Dr. Jack Hayford, writes, *"Saints (are) people who have been made holy in God's eyes through Christ's merit alone. Followers of the Lord are referred to by this phrase throughout the Bible, although it's meaning is developed more fully in the New Testament. Consecration (setting apart) and purity are the basic meanings of the term. Believers are called "saints," (Romans 1:7) and "Saints in Christ Jesus," (Philippians 1:1) because they belonged completely to the One who has provided their sanctification (1 Cor. 1:2; 6:9-11)."* (Hayford's Bible Handbook, page 749)

Consider the following few Scriptures from God's Word:
In 1 Corinthians 1:2, the plain implication is that those who are sanctified in Christ Jesus are the saints.

"... to the saints who are in Ephesus and faithful in Christ Jesus." (Ephesians 1:1)

"...to all the saints in Christ Jesus who are in Philippi..." (Philippians 1:1)

"...to the saints and faithful brethren in Christ who are in Colosse..." (Colossians 1:2)

It is fairly obvious that in each book, Paul the Apostle is writing to the local believers who are disciples of Jesus Christ and living in each respective city. He wasn't writing to dead bodies buried in the cemetery. And he wasn't a spiritist writing to disembodied spirits. The statement has been heard numerous times, *"You must become a saint before you die, because you can't become one after death."* It is appropriate to observe that Biblical terms must not be misapplied by narrow redefinitions that suit the theology or doctrine taught by only one group or denomination.

For example, the Mormons call their organization *"The Church of Jesus Christ of Latter-day Saints."* To them, a saint can only be a baptized member of their church. (Fortunately that's not what the Bible states. Even their world president admitted in July 1999 that the Jesus of the Bible wasn't the same as the Jesus of their church. Christians wondered why this admission took 160 years to be made, since it was fairly obvious.)

The Roman Catholic Church's elevation to "Sainthood" of various people follows a different idea. Because Roman Catholicism is a religion significantly focused on death (that's why they have the body of Jesus Christ still on the cross) their perspective is that dead people are still actively involved with Catholics today. The Bible says this belief is practising necromancy or spiritism/spiritualism, both of which will put the practitioner into the Lake of Fire.

The following may assist, and is a quote from my book **"Unmasking Spiritualism"** I wrote in 1995:
"WHY SO MANY SPIRITUALISTS WITH A CATHOLIC LINK? While I was researching for this book, most of the authors and speakers I studied mentioned the very high proportion of former or current Roman Catholics involved in Spiritualism. As I hadn't thought of any connection prior to this, I decided to investigate. There is plenty of evidence of New Age occultism and other spiritual compromise, such as Freemasonry, in other Christian denominations, (particularly the traditional streams) but those are individual choices

of belief or involvement and not official doctrines. The difference is the official endorsement of some Spiritualist doctrines by the Roman Catholic Church leadership which are inconsistent with the Bible. These include:

The wearing of the Scapular. *The Scapular is nothing more than a good luck charm or fetish, claimed to protect the wearer from the eternal fire of hell. It can do no such thing, for Revelation 20:15 states that the only thing which will prevent any one of us being thrown into the Lake of Fire is to have our name recorded in The Book of Life by God. Our names only get there once we have put our faith in Jesus Christ following repentance from all our sin.*

Purgatory and prayers for those who have died. *There are two destinations for human beings upon death, and both start with H. Those whose names are in The Book of Life will go to* **Heaven***, sometimes called Paradise. The other destination is called* **Hades.** *This is the holding place of the souls and spirits of mankind until the Great White Throne Judgement recorded in Revelation 20. The expectation of Spiritualists, Mormons, Hindus and others of similar opinion is that you can have more than one attempt at life, so you could be improved after death. The [Roman] Catholic view is that the flames of Purgatory will purge a person so they can be improved enough to later enter heaven. These views are disproved in the Bible, for* **"It is appointed once for a man (person) to die and after this comes the judgement,"** *(Hebrews 9:27). Those in Hades will be thrown into the Lake of Fire (see Revelation 20:10-15). There is no other possible destination. Praying for those who have died is a pointless exercise. Anyone who isn't a saint prior to death cannot become one afterwards. The New Testament Epistles were written to "The Saints of..." so they weren't written to dead people but to the living who had placed their faith in Jesus Christ.*

Prayers to dead people, (Mary, other saints) and also angels. *The Bible and other reliable historic sources plainly record that Mary, the mother of Jesus and wife of Joseph, was a virtuous young woman and a virgin prior to the birth of Jesus. There were other women who could have fulfilled God's purposes just as well, but God in His sovereign will decided on Mary. In recognition of her sinful* *state, Mary made the Sin Offering required under the Levitical Law after the birth of Jesus (Luke 2:21-24). This restored her ceremonial cleanliness and gave recognition to God that she too needed a Savior. Since Mary and Joseph had at least six other children (Matthew 13:55-56, Mark 15:40), so she did not remain a virgin.*

*Mary is not God, despite the many attributes given to her by well-meaning but deceived people. She cannot answer prayer. In fact **no dead person can communicate with living human beings according to Jesus** in Luke 16:19-31. Mary is dead, just like every other son and daughter of Adam and Eve. Enoch and Elijah remain the only humans granted the privilege of direct transport into heaven to date. Mary cannot go behind the back of Jesus and appeal directly to the Father since that would cause disunity in the triune Godhead. None of the other "Saints" can answer your prayers either, and angels either do God's bidding, or Satan's. Prayers to Mary or any other dead "Saint" is necromancy. Who do you want to answer your prayers? If God the Father, then we are commanded to pray to Him only through Jesus, (see Acts 7:59, 1 Corinthians 1:2, 1 Timothy 2:5). Any other source is sinful, according to God's word.*

Claimed appearances of the Virgin Mary at Fatima, Medjugorje and elsewhere have no Bible basis. Since these messages from "Our Lady" (of which I have read quite a few) are frequently contrary to the Bible, it must be concluded that these appearances are not Mary the Mother of Jesus who lived 2,000 years ago, but a strong demonic principality deceiving the gullible who do not know their Bibles well enough and so don't know the difference. I don't doubt the sincerity of the people who claim these appearances, but the responsibility for this continued deception lies firmly in the hands of Roman Catholic Church leaders who claim these appearances are authentic. The only command Mary is ever recorded making is recorded in John 2:5, where she told the people, **"Whatever He says to you, do it."** *Obedience to what Jesus says is our only eternal fire insurance."*

So, if you are born again by the Holy Spirit of God, as Jesus stated was essential in John 3:16, then you are a saint. This means you are in covenant and daily relationship with Him, because He is your

Lord and Savior! This describes **who you are in Jesus Christ,** and nothing more.

So, Who is Cursed?

Firstly, because of the Anathemas or Curses adopted at the Council of Trent, and reaffirmed at the Second Vatican Council, everyone with non-Catholic beliefs is cursed.

Secondly, Roman Catholics who agree with the official doctrines of their church are cursed by God as they have surrendered to many anti-Biblical pagan beliefs and doctrines that He opposes. The Papal Pantheon is an occultic snare orchestrated by no less than Satan himself so he has more company in the Lake of Fire.

This writer wants every reader to get right with God on the only terms God offers: Repent from all wrong beliefs and practises, and accept what Jesus Christ really accomplished on that cross at Calvary. He is going to want an account from us when He returns soon. What will your answer be?

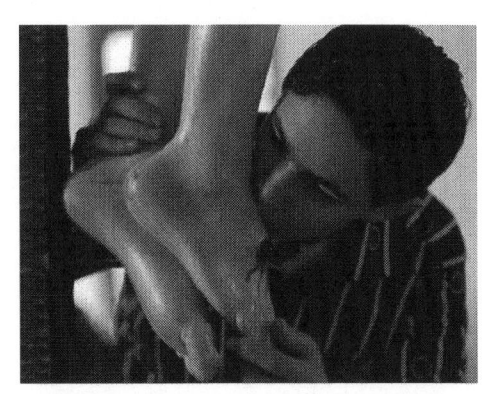

Kissing a statue is a pagan practice, and no way to show love to the real alive Jesus. (see John 14:15)

This is a symbol showing Satan's victory - a dead and powerless Jesus. That fulfilled God's plan, but Jesus rose from the dead and is no longer powerless. In fact, He is returning soon.

PRAYER OF RELEASE FOR EX-ROMAN CATHOLICS & THEIR DESCENDANTS

So, returning to the stated purpose of ministering freedom from ungodly curses and bondages, we suggest and propose the following ministry as the Holy Spirit leads. This follows the same basic pattern as we would minister with those departing cults such as Mormonism, Jehovah's Witnesses, or what has been described as the world's largest operating coven, Freemasonry.

Christians should pray for Roman Catholics without judging them. Bring their sins to God in an attitude of love, petitioning the Father for His mercy, binding in the name of Jesus Christ the spirits of deception, Antichrist, witchcraft and death. Please remember, **"We do not wrestle against flesh and blood (your loved one) but against principalities, against powers, against the rulers of the darkness of this world, against spiritual wickedness in high places," (Ephesians 6:12).** This is a spiritual battle, and should be treated accordingly.

If you were once a member of the Roman Catholic Church or are a descendant of someone who was, we recommend that you pray through this prayer from your heart. Please read it through first so you know what is involved. It is best to pray this aloud with a mature Christian present. We suggest a brief pause following each paragraph to allow the Holy Spirit to show any related issues that may require attention.

"Father God, creator of heaven and earth, I come to you in the name of Jesus Christ your Son. I come as a sinner seeking forgiveness and cleansing from all my sins committed against you, and others made in your image. I honor my earthly father and mother and all of my ancestors of flesh and blood, and of the spirit by adoption and godparents, but I utterly turn away from and renounce all their sins and iniquities. I forgive all my ancestors for the effects of their sins and iniquities on my children and me. I confess and renounce all of my own sins, known or unknown and I accept personally the sacrifice that Jesus gave Himself for me on Calvary. I renounce and rebuke Satan and every spiritual power of his affecting me and my family, in the name of Jesus Christ.

True Holy Creator God, in the name of the True Lord Jesus Christ, in accordance with Jude 8-10; Psalm 82:1 and 2 Chronicles 18, I request you to move aside all Celestial Beings, including Principalities, Powers and Rulers, and to forbid them to harass, intimidate or retaliate against me and all participants in this ministry today.

I also ask that you prevent these beings, of whatever rank, from being permitted to send any level of spiritual evil as retaliation against any of those here, or our families, our ministries, or possessions.

I renounce and annul every covenant made with Death by my ancestors or myself, including every agreement made with Sheol, and I renounce the refuge of lies and falsehoods that have been hidden behind.

In the name of the Lord Jesus Christ I renounce and forsake all ungodly involvement in Roman Catholicism by my ancestors and myself. I renounce every covenant, every blood covenant and every alliance with Roman Catholicism or the spiritual powers behind it made by my family or me. I also renounce and repent of all permission I have ever granted to be deceived, or that was granted by my parents or previous generations without my awareness or consent.

In the name of the Lord Jesus Christ of Nazareth, I renounce every form of ungodly authority and all ungodly power, and I repent for submitting to all ungodly authority. I repent for my loyalty towards the Roman Catholic Church, and its Popes, Cardinals, Archbishops, Bishops, Priests and Nuns when that loyalty and obedience should have been to Jesus Christ. I also repent and renounce any and all impartations I received through any laying on of hands, including by any false priesthood and all religious deception. I especially reject the false teaching and belief in the infallibility of the pope, because only God is true, and every man is a liar, according to Romans 3 verse 4.

I repent for my silence and ignorance about the Roman Catholic Church's historical use of terror, bloodshed, torture, lies, coercion, deception, sexual immorality, fraud, control and manipulation, either directly or through the various Orders of the Church and through the Inquisition. Please heal me from any of these things that have been done to me, or that were done to others with or without my awareness or consent.

In the name of the Lord Jesus Christ of Nazareth, I repent for believing in a church that has kept people from understanding the Holy Bible, when that has the Words of Life. I humbly request to be exempted from the punishment for adding or deducting from God's word recorded in Revelation 22 verses 18 & 19. Please help me understand Your Word the Holy Bible, and to trust it and apply it to my life in a way that will bring glory to Your name, and benefit for my spiritual growth and maturity.

In the name of the Lord Jesus Christ of Nazareth, I reject and repudiate all the beliefs and practises of the Emperor Constantine, especially as Pontifex Maximus, and all the Mithraism and pagan involvement he brought into the church, including their god, "Sol Invictus" - the so-called unconquerable sun, who has been conquered by my Lord Jesus Christ at Calvary. I reject and repudiate the paganism of the Monstrance that was dedicated to the sun gods.

In the name of the Lord Jesus Christ, I also reject and repudiate the pagan gods of the Roman Catholic Church, including Dagon, Osiris, Isis, all the sun gods including Tammuz, Ra and Shamesh, Cybele - the mother-goddess of Rome, Nimrod, Semiramis, Ashtoreth, Molech, Ishtar, Remphan and the fish gods.

In the name of the Lord Jesus Christ of Nazareth I reject and repudiate idolatry of the Pope's title of "Vicar of Christ," as no mortal man can replace the Lord Jesus Christ.

In the name of the Lord Jesus Christ of Nazareth I reject and repudiate the false teaching that Simon Peter is the Rock on which the church is founded. The Lord Jesus Christ is the Rock on which my faith is built, and it was Simon Peter's confession on the deity of Jesus that is the foundation of my faith, and all obedient disciples of Jesus Christ.

In the name of the Lord Jesus Christ of Nazareth, I renounce the pagan syncretism taught alongside true Biblical teaching by the Roman Catholic Church. I reject and repent of all pagan beliefs and practices, and ask to be set free from all such pagan influences in my mind, my will, my emotions, my heart, my conscience, my imagination and my habits.

I choose to forgive everyone who has taught me false doctrine and ungodly religious practices, including the so-called "Sacrifice of the Mass," Transubstantiation. In repenting for all these, I also choose to forgive myself for my active participation or acquiescent acceptance of all such beliefs and practices, in the name of Jesus Christ. I ask for mercy on all who taught me false doctrines and practices and the conviction of the Holy Spirit of the error of their ways, and that they would discover the truth and teach that instead, in Jesus' name.

In the name of the Lord Jesus Christ of Nazareth, I renounce and repent of every form of idolatry, including the idolatry of Holy Mother Church, and any false worship and spiritual adultery I indulged in, even in my ignorance that your Word forbids such practice in Exodus 20 verse 5 and elsewhere. I choose to worship The True Creator God, revealed as Father, Son and Holy Spirit. Please teach me how to worship You in spirit and in truth.

In the name of the Lord Jesus Christ of Nazareth, I repent and renounce every devotion, veneration, worship and idolatry of the Virgin Mary. I recognize and accept that Mary, otherwise know as Miriam, was a good woman chosen by God the Father to bear and bring up the Lord Jesus Christ with her husband Joseph, but that she recognized that she was a sinner needing to make a sacrifice for her personal sins, as confirmed by Luke 2:22-24, and as was the

Scripture-based custom of her day. I also reject and renounce the Co-mediatrix and Intercessory roles of Mary - the mother of Jesus - the Immaculate Conception of Mary, her Perpetual Virginity (despite having at least six other named children) and her Bodily Assumption into Heaven; all of which have no Biblical basis whatever, but are the doctrines of men imposed on Bible-deprived members.

In the name of the Lord Jesus Christ of Nazareth, I renounce the belief in the post-death apparitions of Mary, such as the Madonna, Our Lady of the Rosary, Patroness of Russia, of France, and of the United States of America, The woman clothed with the sun, the Bright and Morning Star, the Lady of Lourdes, the Lady of Fatima, the Lady of Guadeloupe, and the Lady of Medjugorje, I reject all instructions from these and all other similar apparitions because too many of those instructions were contrary to the revealed Word of God, thereby proving the spiritism involved in these. I also reject and renounce as well the other titles including the Queen of Heaven, the Lady of Mercedes, the Lady of the Snows, the Queen of Martyrs, the Queen of Peace, and Mary, Star of the Seas and any other titles attributed to her.

In the name of the Lord Jesus Christ of Nazareth, I repent for praying to dead people, and the necromancy and spiritism that involved, when the Holy Bible in Deuteronomy 18 verse 11 and elsewhere forbids that practice. I ask Your forgiveness for my ignorance of Your clear instructions forbidding this, Heavenly Father. I repent for all belief that dead people can answer my prayers. Please help me learn how to pray in a way that is acceptable to You.

In the name of the Lord Jesus Christ of Nazareth, I repent and renounce all dedication of my life to dead saints, including Mary, and also any dedication to any organization, including the Roman Catholic Church. In cancelling that now, I choose to dedicate my life to the Lord Jesus Christ, the only begotten Son of the Living God and to the purposes of His Kingdom.

In the name of the Lord Jesus Christ of Nazareth, I repent, renounce and cut off all ungodly soul ties and connections with any dead saints that I have been dedicated to or chosen for myself in my ignorance of Your Word, the Holy Bible. I repent for every time I asked any dead saint to pray on my behalf, since this practise is also forbidden in the Bible. I repent for every honor I ever performed to any dead saint where such honor was inconsistent with the Bible and God's revealed will. I ask to be set free from all confusion that praying to saints has caused, and the spiritism this involved, and I request the removal of all harmful influence they have had over my life.

In the name of the Lord Jesus Christ of Nazareth, I repent, and renounce all trust in dedicated objects, including medals, scapulars, statues, sacred heart posters and paintings, the rosary beads, holy water, votive candles, sacred relics and any kissing or bowing to any alleged sacred object or novenas.

In the name of the Lord Jesus Christ of Nazareth, I repent, and renounce all trust in any "sacrament" that does not have a solid Biblical basis, including infant baptism, confirmation, first communion or Eucharist, confession, penance and extreme unction. I also reject and repudiate the anointing with ash on Ash Wednesday because of it's pagan origin of worship to Tammuz, as well as all the paganism of Lent, Easter, Halloween and Christmas.

In the name of the Lord Jesus Christ of Nazareth, I renounce all beliefs that are contrary to Your revealed Word and will, and I ask for You to renew my mind and my heart, and to help me recognize all false teaching and beliefs when I hear or see them. Please protect me from all spiritual deception, regardless of source, in Jesus' name. I also repent for trusting in rituals and objects and attributing power to them, instead of trusting Your love for me and relying on Your power, Your love and Your faithfulness.

In the name of the Lord Jesus Christ of Nazareth, I reject and repent of the shameless use of indulgences to obtain money from members of the Roman Catholic Church by priests by fraud, with false and unsubstantiated promises of quicker release from the imaginary place of the dead called Purgatory, or of the falsely promised cancellation of sins. Lord Jesus, I choose and seek Your assistance by Your Holy Spirit for righteous behavior and motives whenever I deal with issues of money and property.

I reject and repudiate the false claim by Pope John Paul the Second that there is no real hell, as that contradicts the clear teaching from my Lord Jesus Christ from the Holy Bible.

I reject and repudiate the false claim by Pope Francis and other popes that having a personal relationship with Jesus Christ is "dangerous and harmful," because I choose to put my faith and trust in Jesus Christ as my Lord and savior because He is the truth and cannot lie.

In the name of the Lord Jesus Christ of Nazareth, I reject, repent and renounce every form of sexual immorality, perversion, paedophilia, seduction, rape, the killing of babies and the hypocrisy involved in the Roman Catholic by priests and members of other orders over their church members and all others that has been allowed for hundreds of years. I also reject the enforced celibacy of clergy, priests and nuns, as that is not a requirement for ministry to Jesus Christ in the Holy Bible. I repent of every sexual sin that I have committed by thought, word, imagination or deed, in Jesus' name. Holy Spirit, please help me to resist every form of sexual sin and give me a pure heart I so may bring glory to the Living God by my conduct.

Lord God, I thank you for freedom of conscience. In the name of the Lord Jesus Christ of Nazareth, I repent of serving a church that required people to fast through legalism, and that killed people for eating meat during Lent, and I reject the coercion of the Roman Catholic Church priests to live under such legalism. In the name of the Lord Jesus Christ of Nazareth, I repent for every instance where I tried to violate the free will of others.

I thank you Heavenly Father, for the ability to discern the difference between the truth of Your revealed will through the Holy Bible and the doctrines of the Roman Catholic Church where these differ from your Word. In any way I cannot see these differences, please enable me to recognize all error and false teaching. I especially renounce and repent of ever believing the anti-Biblical teachings of transubstantiation, purgatory, and that my salvation may only be obtained by being baptized into membership of the Roman Catholic Church as an infant. In rejecting these false teachings, I choose to trust in the Lord Jesus Christ, and what He did for me on the Cross of Calvary, in His birth, death and resurrection, and ask to have my name recorded in the Lamb's Book of Life (Revelation 21:27). Consequently, I ask to be exempted from the plagues and the rejection by You based on Revelation 22 verses 18 and 19.

Heavenly Father and true holy Creator God, I thank You for helping me live in the freedom that Christ died for me and that is provided by your Holy Spirit. Help me to grow into a strong, mature and fruitful follower of Your Son, the Lord Jesus Christ. Thank you for your goodness, faithfulness, mercy and love towards me. Teach me your ways that I may walk strongly on your paths designed by you for me to walk. Be glorified through my life, and show your love and character through me, that others may see Jesus in me.

In the name of the Lord Jesus Christ of Nazareth, I also renounce, cut off and dissolve in the blood of Jesus Christ every ungodly Soul-tie I or my ancestors have created with other Roman Catholics or participants in occultic groups and actions, and I ask you to send out ministering angels to gather together all portions of my fragmented soul, to free them from all bondages and to wash them clean in the Blood of Jesus Christ, and then to restore them to wholeness to their rightful place within me. I also ask that You remove from me any parts of any other person's soul which has been deposited within my humanity. Thank you Lord for restoring my soul and sanctifying my spirit.

In the name of the Lord Jesus Christ of Nazareth, I renounce and rebuke every evil spirit associated with Roman Catholicism, spiritism, occultic mysticism and all other sins and iniquities involved. Lord Jesus, I ask you to now set me free from all spiritual and other bondages, in accordance with the many promises of the Bible. In the name of the Lord Jesus Christ, I now take the delegated authority given to me and bind every spirit of sickness, infirmity, curse, affliction, addiction, disease or allergy associated with these sins I have confessed and renounced, including every spirit empowering all iniquities inherited from my family.

I exercise the delegated authority from the Risen Lord Jesus Christ over all lower levels of evil spirits and demons which have been assigned to me, and I command that all such demonic beings are to be bound up into one, to be separated from every part of my humanity, whether perceived to be in the body or trapped in the dimensions, and they are not permitted to transfer power to any other spirits or to call for reinforcements.

In the name of the Lord Jesus Christ of Nazareth, I command every evil spirit to leave me now, touching or harming no-one, and go to the dry place appointed for you by the Lord Jesus Christ, never to return to me or my family, and I command that you now take all your memories, roots, scars, works, nests and habits with you. I surrender to God's Holy Spirit and to no other spirit all the places in my life where these sins and iniquities have been.

Holy Spirit, I ask that you show me anything else that I need to do or to pray so that my family and I may be totally free from the consequences of the sins of Roman Catholicism, Witchcraft, Spiritism and all related Paganism and Occultism.

(Pause, while listening to God, and pray as the Holy Spirit leads you.)

Now, dear Father God, I ask humbly for the blood of Jesus Christ, your Son and my Savior, to cleanse me from all these sins I have confessed and renounced, to cleanse my spirit, my soul, my mind, my emotions and every part of my body which has been affected by these sins, in the name of Jesus Christ. I also command every cell in my body to come into divine order now, and to be healed and made whole as they were designed to by my loving Creator, including restoring all chemical imbalances and neurological functions, controlling all cancerous cells, reversing all degenerative diseases, and I sever the DNA and RNA of any mental or physical diseases or afflictions that came down through my family blood lines. I also ask to receive the perfect love of God that casts out all fear, in the name of the Lord Jesus Christ.

I ask you, Lord, to fill me with your Holy Spirit now according to the promises in your Word. I take to myself the whole armor of God in accordance with Ephesians Chapter Six, and rejoice in its protection as Jesus surrounds me and fills me with His Holy Spirit. I enthrone you, Lord Jesus, in my heart, for you are my Lord and my Savior, the source of eternal life. Thank you, Father God, for your mercy, your forgiveness and your love, in the name of Jesus Christ, Amen."

About the Author:
Selwyn R. Stevens,
Ph.D; D.Min.; M.I.S.D.M.; M.E.A.C.M.

is the President of Jubilee Resources International Inc. a New Zealand-based educational and religious organization involved in informing and equipping Christians of all denominations how to reach the lost and deceived in cults, the occult and secret societies such as Freemasonry. Author of over 35 books (and co-author of two), including twelve Best Sellers, an International Speaker (on five continents) and ordained minister. Dr. Stevens is a third-generation preacher, and has been involved in various Christian groups, and also maintains an active interest in national and world affairs and politics. Dr. Stevens is a Foundation Member of the International Society of Deliverance Ministers, founded by Dr. C. Peter Wagner and convened by Dr. William Sudduth of Virginia, USA; and Apostolic Overseer of the Alliance of African Christian Churches & Ministries based in Zambia. Regular Facebook and e-mail teaching and mentoring is also provided to many Christian leaders across Africa, Asia, Caribbean & Latin America, resulting in tens of thousands being equipped for service to the Kingdom of God.

Additional Resources Available by
Selwyn R. Stevens
www.jubileeresources.org (Webshop)

Plus comprehensive range of free tracts to download

Unmasking Freemasonry - Removing the Hoodwink. Written primarily for the wives & families of Masons to explain the curses brought on themselves and their families through the oaths; then learn how to deal with the effects. History & structure are explained simply. A Past Master who read this book immediately resigned from his Lodge. The prayer guidelines from this book are being used by many ministries worldwide. 7th edition with endorsement by C. Peter Wagner. Best Seller *Book, E-book, MP4 & DVD*

Unmasking Mormonism - Who are the Latter-day Saints? Learn about LDS founder Joseph Smith on whose credentials this cult fails Bible tests, the Book of Mormon hoax, Mormon polytheism, true & false priesthood & authority. This book has caused many Mormons to cancel their baptisms & leave to seek the genuine Jesus Christ - the One from the Bible. Best Seller *Book, E-book, MP4 & DVD*

Unmasking the Watchtower - Who are the Jehovah's Witnesses? This asks the questions many J.W.'s are being expelled for daring to ask! Check out the changeable prophecies and man-made doctrines of the Watchtower, the authoritarian leaders & their use of Mind-Control & manipulation of members, how to know the One True God, and how you can witness to and pray for a J.W. effectively. Best Seller *Book, E-book, MP4 & DVD*

Rome's Anathemas: Insights into the Papal Pantheon. This vital book investigates Constantine's divorce of the Jewish roots of the Christian faith and its replacement with paganism; the Council of Trent rejected the Biblical basis of Luther's Reformation and cursed all who disagreed with them. In John, we read of the marriage feast at Cana. Realizing that the wine was gone and that she herself could not do anything, Mary tells Jesus, because He is the only One who could do something. Mary then gives the stewards her last recorded words and only command - one that we must consider for us to be saved. Mary said, *"Whatever He say to you, do it!"* *Book, E-book, MP4 & DVD*

Fatal Faith - the Cult Counterfeit of Christianity. This book explains how cults develop and what patterns to avoid. Key Christian and Cult beliefs are compared with the main active cults. How to handle door-knockers, cult exiting, pre-cult spiritually-abusive churches; and how to protect young people from cults. Major ancient & modern heresies examined. Best Seller.
Book, E-book

The New Age - the Old Lie in a New Package. New Age & Bible beliefs and practices compared, including Reincarnation and Past lives, Astrology, the New Age pseudo Messiah, Self-worship & our Deity-potential. Energy/Life Forces are examined, and the occult involvement of most holistic health gurus. Best Seller
Book, E-book

Discerning the Past to See the End Times: *Islam's Role in the Return of Jesus.* The statue in Nebuchadnezzar's dream, interpreted by Daniel, gives us a clear picture of the various empires that have sought domination of the Middle East and beyond. World events circle around this area of vital interest to God and His people. The Bible is a Middle Eastern book, not a European or American book. The context of the empires of the statue give us vital clues about the Empire of the Beast to come! Best Seller
Book, E-book, MP4 & DVD

Signs & Symbols: Cult, New Age & Occult Insignias & What They Mean. From Ananda Marga, Anarchy, & Ankhs, to Yin & Yang, Yoga & Zodiacs. By popular demand this book has a brief explanation & a Biblical comparison with dozens of insignias. 7th Edition, newly revised. Best Seller
Book, E-book

How to Minister to Change Lives and Communities. This comprehensive & practical training manual is for those who want to do effective ministry. This can include end-of-service and small-group ministry. Topics include Understanding the Spiritual Realm; Empowerment to Serve; Healing of the Body, & the Soul; Deeper Ministry by appointment & referral; & Biblical blessings to release identity and destiny. Best Seller
Book, E-book, MP4 & DVD

The Bible 101. A teaching manual introducing the Bible, explaining clearly it's purposes, origins, history, inspiration, symbolism, translations & versions, moving from milk to meat, study helps, rules of interpretation, and how to study it to get the best understanding.
Book, E-book, & MP4

Fatal Faith - the Cult Counterfeit of Christianity. This book explains how cults develop and what patterns to avoid. Key Christian and Cult beliefs are compared with the main active cults. How to handle door-knockers, cult exiting, pre-cult spiritually-abusive churches; and how to protect young people from cults. Major ancient & modern heresies examined. Best Seller. *Book, E-book*

The New Age - the Old Lie in a New Package. New Age & Bible beliefs and practices compared, including Reincarnation and Past lives, Astrology, the New Age pseudo Messiah, Self-worship & our Deity-potential. Energy/Life Forces are examined, and the occult involvement of most holistic health gurus. Best Seller *Book, E-book*

Discerning the Past to See the End Times: *Islam's Role in the Return of Jesus*. The statue in Nebuchadnezzar's dream, interpreted by Daniel, gives us a clear picture of the various empires that have sought domination of the Middle East and beyond. World events circle around this area of vital interest to God and His people. The Bible is a Middle Eastern book, not a European or American book. The context of the empires of the statue give us vital clues about the Empire of the Beast to come! Best Seller *Book, E-book, MP4 & DVD*

Signs & Symbols: Cult, New Age & Occult Insignias & What They Mean. From Ananda Marga, Anarchy, & Ankhs, to Yin & Yang, Yoga & Zodiacs. By popular demand this book has a brief explanation & a Biblical comparison with dozens of insignias. 7th Edition, newly revised. Best Seller *Book, E-book*

How to Minister to Change Lives and Communities. This comprehensive & practical training manual is for those who want to do effective ministry. This can include end-of-service and small-group ministry. Topics include Understanding the Spiritual Realm; Empowerment to Serve; Healing of the Body, & the Soul; Deeper Ministry by appointment & referral; & Biblical blessings to release identity and destiny. Best Seller *Book, E-book, MP4 & DVD*

The Bible 101. A teaching manual introducing the Bible, explaining clearly it's purposes, origins, history, inspiration, symbolism, translations & versions, moving from milk to meat, study helps, rules of interpretation, and how to study it to get the best understanding. *Book, E-book, & MP4*

Insights into Dying, Death & the Destination Options. This teaching has been providing comfort to many people who have been uncertain of their eternal future. This Biblical approach to a frequently misunderstood issue brings hope with joy, or the timely opportunity to make a crucial correction. *Book, E-book, & MP4*

Dealing with Curses & Generational Iniquities. This teaching offers hope for all Christians that they can be released into the blessings of God and forever leave behind iniquities and curses that have kept them captive, perhaps their whole families for generations. This explains the twelve major curses that people may have operating in their families, and what to do about them. It also includes new material on the curses over Scottish, English, Irish, Welsh and Scandinavian people, plus many other national and ethnic groups. This teaching has been taught in several nations with much fruit for personal, family and community liberty. Best Seller
Book, E-book, MP4 & DVD

Dealing with Demons: *Insights into evil spiritual influences.* This popular teaching provides outstanding insights regarding evil spiritual influences that exist in the world in which we live today, and then goes further to show us what to do about it. Best Seller *Book, E-book, MP4 & DVD*

Insights into Martial Arts, Tai Ch'i TM & Yoga. Much of the western world has seen an explosion of these practices. For many, their involvement has became close to a religion, adopting belief systems, mind sets and practises inconsistent with the teachings of the Bible. Best Seller
Book, E-book, MP4 & DVD

Treated or Tricked - Alternative Health Therapies Diagnosed. Many people are now trying Alternative Health Therapies. This book explains the various medical & spiritual healing methods; investigates whether the "Energy/Life Force" is scientific or spiritual; and describes almost 80 different Alternative Therapies, from Aromatherapy to Zone therapies. Also examines reasons why some are not healed & how to overcome these failures Biblically. Co-authored with Dr. Badu Bediako, (former Assoc. Professor of BioChemistry.) Best Seller *Book, E-book, MP4 & DVD*

How to Recognize the Voice of God. How does God communicate to His people? How will you know when it is Him speaking to you? This very practical teaching has already helped many.
Book & DVD

Additional Resources Available by
Selwyn R. Stevens
www.jubileeresources.org (Webshop)
Plus comprehensive range of free tracts to download

Printed in Poland
by Amazon Fulfillment
Poland Sp. z o.o., Wrocław